The Economics of Online Gaming

I0033631

The Economics of Online Gaming

A Player's Introduction to
Economic Thinking

Andrew Wagner

BEP BUSINESS EXPERT PRESS

The Economics of Online Gaming:
A Player's Introduction to Economic Thinking
Copyright © Business Expert Press, LLC, 2020.

All rights reserved. No part of this publication may be reproduced, stored in a retrieval system, or transmitted in any form or by any means— electronic, mechanical, photocopy, recording, or any other except for brief quotations, not to exceed 250 words, without the prior permission of the publisher.

First published in 2020 by
Business Expert Press, LLC
222 East 46th Street, New York, NY 10017
www.businessexpertpress.com

ISBN-13: 978-1-94858-091-5 (paperback)
ISBN-13: 978-1-94858-092-2 (e-book)

Business Expert Press Economics and Public Policy Collection

Collection ISSN: 2163-761x (print)
Collection ISSN: 2163-7628 (electronic)

Cover image licensed by Ingram Image, StockPhotoSecrets.com
Cover and interior design by S4Carlisle Publishing Services Private Ltd., Chennai, India

First edition: 2020

10 9 8 7 6 5 4 3 2 1

Printed in the United States of America.

Abstract

This book is made from the connections that the author saw when he compared his experience inside a video game with what he learned through a formal study of economic theory. Set in the Massively Multiplayer Online Role-Playing Game (MMORPG) of Eternal Lands, it follows the true story of Mr.Mind, a gamer who builds a business inside the game world that he calls RICH. This business grows from a small startup to an unregulated natural monopoly that abuses its market power by intentionally losing money to drive competitors out of business. RICH becomes so influential that it breaks the market process with a unique case of regulatory capture. Through this story, the book demonstrates how economic thinking is absorbed by experimenting inside an online video game.

The book covers some basic economic concepts such as definitions that describe pieces and features of an economic system; how decisions are influenced by time and money; how supply and demand can change, and how those changes affect a market; and different forms of market structures and their effects on competition.

The book also covers more unique economic issues like when boycotting succeeds and fails; the collapse of a cartel; employee loyalty; how a "bad" reputation can actually improve sales; how regulations can have unintended consequences; and who gets left behind when a market changes.

Beyond the basic economic ideas that are explicitly addressed, there are more general themes threaded throughout the book: how people respond to incentives; having the right people make decisions for a group; how different markets are connected; and the value of changing your mind when faced with new information.

Each of these topics begins with the context of a story and continues with an explanation of the economic theory behind it, finishing with a relevant real-world connection. It supports economic theory in an emotional way that cannot be shared through math or charts or graphs.

Keywords

video games; video game economics; scarcity; market dynamics; market structure; market competition; market power; MMO; MMORPG; reputational capital; predatory pricing; price dumping; price controls; monopoly; regulatory capture

Contents

Preface

This book is about an online game, but it's not just for people who play games. It is written for everyone who is curious (or anxious!) about economics, and anyone who enjoys a fantasy novel should be able to appreciate some part of the story. Parts of this book can also benefit game or simulation designers, policy creators, and business strategists.[1]

We are not taking a comprehensive look at every economic concept. This is only an introduction to a way of thinking that spends more time on the ideas than on the numbers. The full story contains more drama than I could include in an educational version, and the data that I found could cover many more pages, but it has enough to show that economics can be fun when applied in the right places.

Each chapter of this book has two parts: the story and the economics. And there are many ways to read it. Anyone who considers economics to be boring should start with Appendix A. This will spoil most of the story, but it should make the rest of the book sound more interesting. (Students who are reluctant to read this book should also know that getting better at economics can help you get better at video games.) Educators who are considering this book for their classes should start with Appendix B. This appendix is an outline of the concepts this book will cover. It is also a source of ideas on how each chapter can facilitate a meaningful introduction to economic thinking. Table 1 summarizes the primary economic theme for each chapter (there are many secondary themes):

---

[1]It also includes ideas that may be helpful for developing an investment philosophy, but nothing in this book should be considered investment advice.

Table 1 Economic theme by chapter

Primary economic theme	
Chapter 1	Types of goods
Chapter 2	Inputs and outputs
Chapter 3	Perfect competition
Chapter 4	Reputational capital
Chapter 5	Monopolistic competition
Chapter 6	Cartels
Chapter 7	Vertical integration
Chapter 8	Normal goods and inferior goods
Chapter 9	Supply and demand shifters
Chapter 10	Regulatory barrier to entry
Chapter 11	Boycott
Chapter 12	Anti-competitive behavior
Chapter 13	Opportunity cost
Chapter 14	Regulatory capture
Chapter 15	Principal/agent problem
Chapter 16	Monopoly to oligopoly
Chapter 17	Video game design (Incentives)

For anyone who has enough time and interest, the easiest and most entertaining way to read this book is to read it twice. Start by reading the story on its own and skipping the economics. When you can follow the story as an action and a reaction, read the story again with the economics included (or skim the story and focus on the economics). The context of a story makes the economics easier to understand, and reading the story first will make the economics easier to remember.

This book is built on research that came from 3 years of living inside an online game and more than 10 years of reviewing what I saw. It's a story based in a medieval fantasy-themed online game world named Eternal Lands, but it's a true story about real people who make real choices. The questions that interested me while I lived inside this game were all about connecting the real world to the game world. What I found, through an informal experiment that started as a misunderstanding, was that economic rules are universal. The economy inside an online game can be described using the same economic models that explain the real world. But the most powerful insight was that I saw how these rules shaped the behavior of players within the game before I ever fully understood the economics. This led to my belief, backed by my own experience, that the right game can be a useful tool for introducing the economics that explain how the world works.

I did not always consider my experience to be noteworthy. I played the game in high school, but the first time I shared the whole story in the real world was at a Christmas party in 2007 during my sophomore year of college. It was a way for me to explain why I chose to study economics. I never intended to write any of it down, and I hadn't even planned to keep any records of it. It was such an afterthought that I had destroyed most of my data only a month earlier. I never expected that my informal experiment could ever be as useful as real-world economic research. It was only valuable to me as a way to make economics easier to understand, and I did not see how it could be useful for anyone else. But my classmates insisted that I put it on paper.

I spent the next 9 months recovering as much of my data as I could find and reviewing everything I knew about the video game world that you're about to see—the culture, the markets, and how they shifted over time; my influence and the game creator's changes; and how a game world can be connected to the real world. The result was an enthusiastically written paper of over 120 pages (single spaced). It was not a masterpiece.

When I finished my writing, I did what I thought any serious writer would do. I found a professor who didn't know me, and I knocked on his office door. I was a junior in college.

The professor's initial appraisal can be summarized by the one phrase that he kept repeating: "This is *insane!*" But, after he read it, he recommended that I make a shorter version as an academic paper. I decided to take his advice.

By the time I became a senior, I cut my manuscript to less than 20 pages. This was short enough to read, but long enough to show the basics behind the economy that I studied, and clear enough to understand that economics is more interesting when it's put in the form of a story or a game. I titled my paper "The Economics of Video Game Design" and used it as my senior project.

If I had stopped there, I could have called the project a surprising success. But I continued to press the question of whether a study about a video game can be as useful as real-world research. A few weeks after I completed my senior project, I quickly typed out a very simple one-sentence abstract: "This paper describes the economic modeling required to have a viable economy within an online computer game." Then I submitted it to a conference hosted by the Federal Reserve Bank of Dallas.

The reviews were mixed. My paper did not have as much math as the average economist would include, but the selection committee felt that my project was in the spirit of their goals, and they offered me a place in their schedule.

The time slot that the conference awarded to me was actually the best one that they could offer. It was the only presentation that came in the hour before lunch, a rare position that made my topic a central theme. My research, based on a story that I almost threw away, from data that I almost erased, was considered just as valuable as heavy economic research. It was beyond unexpected. My presentation was so well-received that it led to an offer that I could not refuse—a "full ride" for a master's degree in economics.[2]

Over the past decade, I've made more than a dozen major revisions to this text. Most of this work has been on my own, with occasional comments from readers, but I have to thank my first editor, Elisabeth Chretien, for posing some hard questions. I am also grateful for the encouragement and insightful comments from Professor Dan Kuester, Director of Undergraduate Studies in Economics at K-State, and Professor Ken Brown, Economics Department Head at Missouri State. And thanks to Phil Romero, at Business Expert Press, for providing the support I needed to get this project published. And, of course, I'll never forget the anonymous professor who agreed to read my first draft.

There were also people involved with the story who were essential to the development of my experiments within Eternal Lands. I will use their names as they are known within the game: The first is my brother, robo2917, who convinced me to be his RICH cofounder. Among the other significant contributors, including hundreds of RICH members, are seanodonnell, gadai, trollson, Lunksnark, SiKiK, jhunLEMON, JimmyTheSaint, Protolif, SplargaMan, and Eon_Schmidt. They are not

---

[2] I was the first Kansas State student to attend this conference. Thanks to this start, and the support of the Economics Department, K-State has sent more than 50 students to the Dallas Fed ESP.

all mentioned in this version of the story, but they were all valuable advisors who influenced the strategies that I used. Many of them are still good friends, but I must apologize for anyone I cannot remember.

The story would not exist without the players who assisted with my plans, but it could not have been reconstructed without the players who made heroic efforts to preserve the game's culture. Entropy deserves credit for creating the game and keeping it active long enough for me to extract the information I needed, but I owe just as much to the players who were speaking in the moment, sharing how they felt at the time, even when they were my rivals. A large part of the story can be restored by this public record alone, and it's almost as good as reading from a private diary.[3] The players with a more neutral analysis, who faithfully recorded the game's economic shifts and market history, were exceptionally valuable for this project, particularly bkc56 and trollson's commentaries on the economy, Torg's market price list, flinto's cost calculation spreadsheet, and SiKiK's bot price spreadsheet (a file that took me 8 years to find and recover). Where possible, I verified or adjusted for the prices and conditions that were in effect at each point in the story. It was enormously difficult to secure accurate and consistent data for such a small game with a decaying Internet history, but I saved the most important features of the story that I was able to find.

The focus of this project has evolved over time, and more reflection has led to a more sympathetic tone. It has also led to the realization that it's impossible to repeat the conditions and the outcome that I experienced within this story, because my character of Mr.Mind is the only player in any online game who became this influential without directly joining a development team. But there is one thing that has not changed. Every step, from the beginning of the game to the end of this book, started with one major motivation: "Why not try something new, just to see what happens?" I would call it an excuse to continue. Sometimes passion is mistaken for insanity.

---

[3]Many of these players are quoted throughout this book. In some cases, I have made minor spelling corrections and/or minor grammar fixes while preserving the context and voice of the original quote. Where misspellings and grammar choices appeared intentional, I left them as they were. Special thanks to Entropy for providing permission to use quotes from the message board.

Introduction

There is a quote that I saved once—an anonymous comment on an article about economics—that captures the theme of this book. It said:

> Economics remains an esoteric subject, bathed in arcane mathematics and beyond comprehension to most. If economists cannot make economics simple enough for the common man to understand, then its usefulness as a guide to policy making is seriously sullied. It's about time they came down from their Ivory Towers and mingled with the masses.

This is the challenge facing anyone who studies economics. Understanding economics is hard, and simplifying economic ideas is even more difficult. Even if those conditions are met, economics still has to overcome its reputation as being one of the most boring subjects to study. I've seen economics majors struggle with it. For example, I once took an advanced economics class with only five students. The professor started one of his lectures by asking for a vote on canceling the next class. *Three* students raised their hands. The other two were already asleep! This is how most people feel about economics.

I don't live in the Ivory Towers of the mathematicians who research economics. But I've been a persistent visitor, and I've seen the models that they use. From the outside, it's almost offensive to see an equation that claims to describe how a person—a person with free will and feelings—decides what to do with their time and their money. At the same time, we have to accept that, on a basic level, consistency and predictability make life easier, and most people will try to spend their time and money in a way that offers them the most happiness (they might not always make the right choice to reach that goal, but that is basically what they are trying to do). We all have our own rules for how we expect people to behave. The difference is that economists try to make sure that they can support their predictions using research, and they formalize these rules into equations.

Using Video Games for Teaching and Researching[1]

Equations are a helpful way of looking at the world, but they may not be enough to understand what economists are trying to say. Economists use numbers and graphs, but there is a story behind these numbers, and there is drama inside the way the graphs move. My study of economic theory was supported by my experience inside an online video game world, a world where I could see the people behind the equations. Almost everything that I saw in this game could be reimagined as a context for abstract economic ideas. Whenever I heard a new economic rule, I could replay a scenario in my mind where I saw this rule applied in the game world. I lived the economics before I learned the economics, and that made it much easier to understand. Swords and shields made for more powerful examples than guns and butter.

I started this game with a set of rules based on how I expected other players to play the game. When my expectations were wrong, I updated them. It was a process of exploration that avoided the burden of complicated equations. I did not need math to learn the economics; I only needed a demonstration of how the economics worked. My game experience of testing new ideas and making mistakes made the theory easier to understand. By the time I started reading the textbooks, I had already seen most of the rules. The textbooks only changed the words that I used to talk about them. This can be true for anyone.

The rules of economics can be applied anywhere, and video games provide an easily adjustable system that can demonstrate many of these different applications. The content of this book is limited to one group within one game, but the bigger idea is how video games can help people learn how to solve difficult problems without the fear of failure. They are places where people can get relevant real-world experience that would never be available in any other way, and this experience can powerfully reinforce other methods of teaching. Video games are also a useful translation tool. The game can *show* how something works and provide a real experience. This is far more effective than any detailed

---

[1] This segment is heavily influenced by a blending of ideas from Gee (2007), McGonigal (2011), and Castronova (2005).

description (one cannot learn how to dance just by reading about how to dance!). When learning is just a cycle of memorizing and forgetting, the students who stand out are often the ones who simply memorize better than the others. They might do well on an exam, but the real world does not challenge people this way. The real world is much more like a game's experience than a school. It's nice to have both the information and a way of analyzing it, but it is much better to learn *how* to think rather than *what* to think, because thinking should be changed when information changes. Recognizing behavioral patterns is one of the most significant skills that games can encourage, a critically important feature of economic studies.

A good game starts with the basic skills. It allows players to improve on these skills by experimenting inside the game world and keeping what works. And it takes time to understand how a system works. But when a player becomes an expert at their level, they can easily move up to something more advanced where the rules have changed. A good game will continue adding new challenges, and players will be forced to respond by changing their routines. They can practice, then master, then move up to another level. And the player will stay interested as long as they feel like the rewards of moving up are worth it. This is exactly what good teachers are trying to do. Leslie Grimm, The Learning Company cofounder (a company that made educational games), summarized this approach. She said, "The programs I designed were done to lead kids towards the answer, rather than punish them for not getting it the first time round." (Cain 2018).

The real power of a game comes from the entertainment, a quality that this book attempts to capture. Games provide an environment that instantly tells the player how they're doing, and they offer challenges and rewards that match the player's skill. When the rewards feel like they're worth the effort, the players want to keep playing. Something that is entertaining is also easier to remember and easier to understand. It's a way to fool yourself into enjoying the boring subjects. In his "last lecture," the late Carnegie Mellon Professor Randy Pausch described this idea as "the head fake." You think you're just having fun, but you're actually learning something too (Pausch 2007). This idea is usually aimed at grade school subjects—with games like Reader Rabbit—but it can also work with business and economics. There are already major universities that use video games for this purpose; about

300 universities, colleges, and business schools have used educational economics games created by a company called MobLab.[2]

This idea is not about replacing teachers. It's about helping good teachers become better teachers. Teaching becomes more effective when students earn rewards for building on what they've already learned, and when they are encouraged to work beyond just doing what they're told to do. Students also have to be given the right tools, and games can be one of these tools; none of the world's major theories were uncovered without the background knowledge needed to build up to them, and the games can help to fill it in. Games can make a theory easier to understand because they are engaging and entertaining, but we still need the teachers to explain why it works.

The exciting part is when game environments are designed around an economic simulation that requires the player to learn the economics to get better at the game. Even when they are not specifically designed for this purpose, almost every online game has markets and an economy. They are simulated markets, but they function based on real economic rules. These economic decisions all start with the idea of looking at how to make choices with limited resources. Everything beyond this idea only specifies which resources or adds complexity to the model. It stretches to every level, from the individual decisions that each player makes, to the group decisions behind how these players organize, all the way up to the viewpoint of the world's creator who builds the system that influences these choices. With enough imagination, it all translates into the real world. It's the most powerful teaching tool there is.

Online games also have a useful human quality for researchers in behavioral science. Why did a player choose this role? How did players respond to changes in the game? What caused these reactions? Does this make sense for the real world? Human behavior cannot always be summarized by a neat equation. General rules can be produced, but these depend on assumptions about the way people make decisions. These assumptions do not always reflect reality, because the environment is dynamic and heavily interconnected, and people do not always make consistent rational choices. A simple multiplayer game can be an easy way to observe

---

[2] MobLab, personal communication, July 10, 2019.

these issues. Even if we can't uncover anything new, these game simulations are still useful for describing different pieces of the real world.

A Brief History of Simulation Games

The influence on my views of economic thinking began with a type of strategy game called economic simulation games. They function around a set of rules that simulates a model economy (such as SimCity 2000, Railroad Tycoon II, and Capitalism II). These games include a wide range of business and economic ideas, from management to marketing, and some even have a functioning stock market. They make their purpose—running a business or city—obvious from the title.

The history of these games goes back much farther than my own experience. Classic board games such as Chess are sometimes considered simulation games, but the widely accepted genesis of today's popular multiplayer simulation games started with Dungeons & Dragons (D&D) in 1974, a fantasy role-playing game (RPG). An RPG is a game where players control a character in a fictional world and make decisions that create a story, like an interactive novel (Schick 1991).

D&D is played with pen and paper. A worldwide network of computers first became involved around 1978–1980 with the introduction of MUD1, a type of game called a Multi-User Dungeon or Multi-User Domain (MUD), an online text-based RPG. The MUD games, when combined with computer graphics and a huge number of players, evolved into today's major online games, known as Massively Multiplayer Online Role-Playing Games (MMORPG or just MMO). The first recognized MMO was Meridian 59, released by 3DO in 1996. Since then, hundreds of MMOs have been created, but only a few are worth listing here, in Table I.1. Fantasy is by far the most common theme for an MMO (Mulligan and Patrovsky 2003; Olson 2014).

Most MMOs are endlessly addictive games for many players. They are a subset of simulation games that are different from the more basic strategy games because there is often no concrete objective (the player chooses who they want to be and what they want to reach for) and no way to "finish" the game's story; the story itself is made by what the players do, and it continues as long as there are players to play it. Even in the many cases

Table I.1 Noteworthy MMOs

MMO	Creator	Year	Theme	Known for
Ultima Online	Electronic Arts	1997	Medieval fantasy	The first major commercially supported MMO. Defined the player interactions for all future MMOs. Briefly the largest MMO in the world until it was overtaken by Lineage.
Lineage	NCsoft	1998	Medieval fantasy	First MMO to reach over one million subscribers. Largest MMO in Asia and the world until it was overtaken by World of Warcraft.
EverQuest	Sony	1999	Fantasy	Largest MMO in North America until it was overtaken by World of Warcraft.
RuneScape	Jagex	2001	Medieval fantasy	One of the most accessible MMOs because it can be played inside a web browser. Still the world's largest free MMO.
EVE Online	CCP Games	2003	Science fiction	High-stakes economic warfare. Large "corporation" space battles. Has an in-house economist who publishes reports about the game.
World of Warcraft	Blizzard	2004	Fantasy	Deeply engaging storytelling. Large multiplayer "raids" against monsters. Made MMOs easy for casual players to enjoy. Still the world's largest MMO and the most popular MMO ever made.

where there is a limit to how powerful a player can become, there are still more places to explore and more people to meet. As virtual worlds, they mirror the real world, and they generate a dynamic "in-game economy" directed by the interaction of the players within the game. The difference is that the economic simulation games generally only work with a fixed set of predictable rules, because they have one human player and many predictable computer players; MMOs also include the somewhat unpredictable human nature, because they have many human players trying different strategies.

My first exposure to these online worlds was in middle school, where I played RuneScape.[3] RuneScape is a simple medieval fantasy-themed MMO with fighting, mining, blacksmithing, cooking, and a wide range of other skills to train. I only played RuneScape for a few months before

---

[3] If I was in middle school today, I would probably be playing Minecraft.

someone stole my game account, but it helped me figure out how to develop a successful nonviolent MMO character. It also inspired the curiosity that created this book.

Eternal Lands

In high school, my summer free time encouraged me to find a new game. I looked for something like RuneScape, and what I found was Eternal Lands (EL). EL was created in 2002 by a man who calls himself Entropy, or "Teh G0d" of Eternal Lands.[4] His version of the creation story is very technical, but he was clear about the purpose of his game:

> I had this dream about making my *own* game, a game where a lot of players can build houses, farms, grow animals and crops, have elections, go to war against CPU controlled entities or other cities, have pirates, looters, attacking the travelers, etc. and it was supposed to be some sort of medieval simulator. (Privantu 2004)

EL did not expand as fast as Entropy hoped, but his design was good enough to be sustainable. It was very similar to RuneScape—it had a sensible skill system, a functional user interface, and a huge area to explore. It was also one of the few games that could connect players on Macintosh computers, Linux computers, and Windows computers (this was probably the most important feature).

EL's early economic history was one of *hyperinflation*. Hyperinflation is an extreme case of inflation where prices are rising out of control. The first markets were not created until October of 2003, but by the end of 2003, silver bars were flooding the market and making everyone wealthy. The price for titanium bars flew past 6,000 gold coins, and only went higher from there. The prices for other common items also exploded. Players from the early years of EL recalled that wolf fur, something that was easy to get (just find a wolf and kill it), could sell for more than 6,000 gold coins. Table I.2 below is a snapshot of what the market for weapons and armor looked like at the time.

---

[4] "Teh G0d" (the god of EL) is what he called himself.

Table I.2 The first EL manufacturing market

Item	Price
Armor	
Leather gloves	1,000
Leather boots	5,000
Leather pants	5,000
Leather torso	10,000
Iron chainmail	20,000
Shields	
Wooden shield	10,000
Iron shield	35,000
Steel shield	90,000
Weapons	
Iron sword	15,000
Iron broad sword	30,000
Steel long sword	60,000
Steel two-edged sword	130,000
Titanium steel short sword	250,000
Titanium steel long sword	900,000
Titanium steel serpent sword	1,900,000

At the time, because of limitations in the programming, players could not keep more than 65,535 coins in their storage. Gold coins also had a weight limit based on the character's attributes, and most players were unable to carry more than a few thousand gold coins. To fix these problems, the game included platinum coins that were worth 1,000 gold coins each, just to enable players to trade with each other. Inflation was completely out of control.[5]

I never saw this part of the EL history. Entropy reset the entire game sometime between April and June of 2004, by

---

[5] Money should serve three functions: be a unit of account (to be able to compare prices); be a medium of exchange (to be able to buy things easily without having to trade); and be a store of value (price changes should be consistent and reliable). These gold coins were failing as both a medium of exchange and a store of value. They were not easy to trade and they did not hold their value.

- erasing everyone's skills and items, forcing every player to start over from the beginning;
- removing two zeroes from the price of most items, resetting the value of gold coins;
- setting fixed prices in a way that prevented inflation; and
- making gold coins weightless, making it easier to trade.

As Table I.3 shows, it was as if the inflation had never happened.[6]

Table I.3 Prices reset

Item	Old price	New price
Armor		
Leather gloves	1,000	50
Leather boots	5,000	90
Leather pants	5,000	110
Leather torso	10,000	100
Iron chainmail	20,000	200
Shields		
Wooden shield	10,000	100
Iron shield	35,000	800
Steel shield	90,000	2,600
Weapons		
Iron sword	15,000	270
Iron broad sword	30,000	500
Steel long sword	60,000	850
Steel two-edged sword	130,000	3,300
Titanium steel short sword	250,000	6,500
Titanium steel long sword	900,000	40,000
Titanium steel serpent sword	1,900,000	190,000

---

[6] As a preview to the type of comparisons we will see throughout the book, consider one of the most famous cases of hyperinflation, the Weimar Republic in Germany from 1918 to 1923, where the country literally printed money in its effort to make war reparations payments from WWI. There was so much money in the system that the bank notes became worthless, and German residents needed wheelbarrows just to buy their bread. The German government ended this hyperinflation by scrapping the old currency and replacing it with a new one from 1923 to 1925, cutting nine zeros from the value of the bank notes. While the causes are different, the effects of Germany's hyperinflation were remarkably similar to the EL version of hyperinflation (Fergusson 2010; Goodman 1981; Llewellyn, Southey, and Thompson 2014).

By the time I found the game, sometime in the summer of 2004, it was healthy, and it had already attracted about 2,000 to 3,000 players. The players came for the features, but they stayed for the social world. EL was different from other MMOs because it took a few more steps to install the game and start learning how to play, which discouraged most of the immature and impatient players. This meant that the average player was much older and more mature, but it also limited how big the game could become. And, as a smaller game with a short history, new players could catch up to the leaders if they learned a good strategy.

Like other MMOs, players could choose what they wanted to be. For example, they could be a fighter or an alchemist. They could also choose how they wanted to be known. This usually meant the difference between choosing to be a nice player or a mean player. But, as we will see, every part of EL was also layered with a coating of untamed game design that encouraged players to test new ways of playing an MMO. There was enough freedom, and enough of an economic imbalance, for me to look at the game and think about what I could learn from it. From that perspective, I would call Eternal Lands the greatest game that I have ever played. This is the story of how I played it, why I tested it, and what I found when I reviewed the results.

PART I

The Market

CHAPTER 1

Hunting Rabbits, Picking Flowers

I poofed into Eternal Lands (EL) as MrMind178, a 16-year-old high school student, with two of my younger brothers, j_wag17, who was 14, and robo2917, only 12, sometime in the summer of 2004. We landed in Isla Prima (IP), the small "newbie island" where players are introduced to the game. The game did not have any guides that were easy to follow, and it did not explain what we were supposed to do. It didn't even tell us how to ask for help. The best we could do was explore the area and try to figure it out on our own.

After a few hours of walking around, occasionally chasing down the small animals that lived on the island, we eventually went inside a village tavern. Inside the tavern was a tavern keeper. The tavern keeper was a nonplayer character (NPC). An NPC in EL was an automated character (very similar to a robot) created by Entropy and controlled by his programming. It would buy and sell whatever Entropy commanded it to buy and sell, and it would use whatever prices Entropy chose. What we discovered, while talking with this NPC, was that the IP tavern keeper would buy rabbit fur and raw meat for one gold coin each. We could make money, one gold coin at a time, by hunting rabbits.

We spread out around the island and claimed our own hunting areas. It was a simple business: Hunt rabbits, collect gold coins; hunt more rabbits, collect more gold coins. Our scheme was painfully slow, but it was the best process that we could come up with on our own. And no matter how many rabbit furs we sold, the NPC would never change its price. One rabbit fur was always one gold coin.

Hunting rabbits was an extremely slow task because healing items were not widely available to new players. As veterans of RuneScape, we were accustomed to having our health restored when we ate the food that we harvested from the village vegetable garden. But EL was different in a subtle way. Eating food only restored the character's *energy*, which slowly drained as the character's health recovered. It took a long time to restore health after a big fight, and we did not have a way to make it happen any faster. The tavern keeper was not selling any health potions, and we did not have the skill to make them.

The health regeneration took so long that our impatience compelled us to take more risks with our fighting. We would fight rabbits and beavers, and sometimes the more powerful deer, until our health was almost gone. Then, if we couldn't win, we would try to run away at the very last second. It was inevitable that trying to run away would eventually fail, and jwag_17 was the first to die, killed by a deer.

When a player died in the game, they dropped a random amount of what they were carrying, and they were sent to a place called the Underworld, a maze that looked a lot like the inside of a volcano. It took a long time to escape. After 5 minutes of walking through the Underworld maze, j_wag17 finally poofed back into IP, but most of his stuff was gone and his health was barely above zero. Dying was a huge cost for the small benefit from fighting small animals, and we scaled back our risk to keep income steady. Dying added more time than waiting to heal.

It took about 3 days for three newbies to save 200 gold coins. We thought it was a lot, at least enough to buy something, so we went looking for something to buy. It was the first time that we deliberately explored beyond the newbie island. Following the game's map, we took the only boat on IP to the heavily wooded White Stone (WS) region and stopped in what was called the Lakeside Village. This is where we found the blacksmith shop, the perfect place to buy new hunting gear.

The blacksmith NPC had some nice weapons and armor for sale, but the only thing that we could afford to buy was a wooden shield, and that was 100 gold coins. *The cheapest item on the list was more than a day's work!* It was too much effort and not enough reward. The game was too slow. Everything was too expensive, and there was not an easy way to learn how to play. We had to do something different, so we changed our strategy:

j_wag17, discouraged by a lack of direction, decided to quit the game; robo2917 left to explore other parts of the game; and I went back to the island in search of a better way to make money.

A few days later, a friendly player approached me with some advice. He insisted that he knew the fastest way to make money in the game, and all I had to do was follow him to find it. So I did.

We sailed across the continent to a place called the Valley of the Dwarves (VOTD). It was the game's main market and storage area, and it was packed with players. Just inside the city's entrance, to the side of an open storage area, sitting on crumbling white wall, was a purple lilac bush. That lilac bush, the player explained, was the fastest way to make money in the game. By harvesting the lilacs and selling them to a nearby flower shop, I could make money in the same way that I made money with the rabbit furs. But what made this method special was the fact that the flower shop was only three steps away from the bush. The way the game was designed, the bush would never run out of flowers no matter how many flowers I picked, and the flower shop would never run out of money no matter how many flowers I sold. It was an effortless way to make money! Harvest flowers, sell flowers; harvest more flowers, sell more flowers. I made as many gold coins in less than an hour picking flowers as my brothers and I made from 3 days of rabbit hunting!

Before the mysterious traveler disappeared, he made sure to show me to the market channel. This, he told me, was where I could trade with other players and bargain for the best prices. Buying and selling with an NPC was possible, but trading with other people would always be a better option, and it came with the potential to make a lot more money. He preferred to make his money by buying iron helms at a low price and reselling them at a higher price. He told me that the market prices move up and down in predictable ways, everything is worth a range of prices, and that I could make money simply by trading. I was not rich enough to afford taking that kind of risk, but I liked the idea of becoming one of the market suppliers. The game did not have an objective, and I was fine with making it all about the money.

A few weeks of picking flowers gave me enough money to start making my own swords and armor to sell in the market. It was a slow process: First, I would walk across a place called the Desert Pines (DP), a map that was top-half forest and bottom-half desert, separated by a river down the middle. There, I would collect sulfur and make fire essences (magic items necessary to make iron and steel bars) with flowers that I gathered in VOTD. Then I would harvest coal and iron in the DP mines, hauling heavy loads from the mines at the edges of the desert to the storage in the center. When I was done with the heavy lifting, I would sit inside the storage and convert it all into iron and steel bars that became weapons and armor. It was a simple process:

1. Make fire essences.
2. Harvest coal and iron ore.
3. Make iron and steel bars.
4. Manufacture swords and armor.
5. Sell swords and armor to other players.

This was the beginning of my EL business career, and the basis behind the structure of the entire game.

The most basic skills in the game were *attack* and *defense*, the fighting skills. Whenever a player made a hit on an enemy, they would gain attack experience. Whenever a player dodged an attack from an enemy, they gained defense experience. When a player killed their enemy, whether that meant an animal, monster, or sometimes even another player, they would be able to pick up whatever that enemy dropped on the ground. Sometimes these items were valuable, and they often included gold coins. Almost every player began their EL career by hunting rabbits in IP, but, as they leveled up, they could fight against more powerful enemies and earn more valuable rewards. The fighting skills were the most intuitive because they only required clicking on an enemy to begin fighting, or, in some places, waiting for a hostile enemy to attack. The fighters were the biggest buyers of weapons and armor.

For producers/sellers, it started with *harvesting*, the other most basic skill in the game. Harvesting allowed players to gather basic ingredients such as such as flowers, minerals, and metal ore. The basic ingredients from harvesting were used in the *alchemy* skill to produce the next step of items, which included magic essences and metal bars. The magic essences and metal bars were used in many different skills to finish the process:

- The *magic* skill used magic essences for casting magic spells.
- The *summoning* skill combined magic essences and animal parts (bones, raw meat, and animal furs) to summon animals or monsters.
- Magic essences combined with flowers made potions using the *potions* skill.
- Metal bars and magic essences were combined to make swords and armor with the *manufacturing* skill, and special rings and medallions using the *crafting* skill.

The potions, weapons and armor, and special rings and medallions were the final products ready to be sold to the final customers. The final customers were the players who focused on their fighting skills, the *attack* and *defense* skills. If we come full circle, the attack and defense skills were the centerpiece of the game. Every other skill either directly or indirectly supported those two skills. Manufactured and crafted items could increase a fighter's effectiveness. Potions and magic skills provided the ability to heal quickly. And summoning gave fighters the ability to create their own monsters to protect themselves or to train their fighting skills. Figure 1.1 shows this connection.[1]

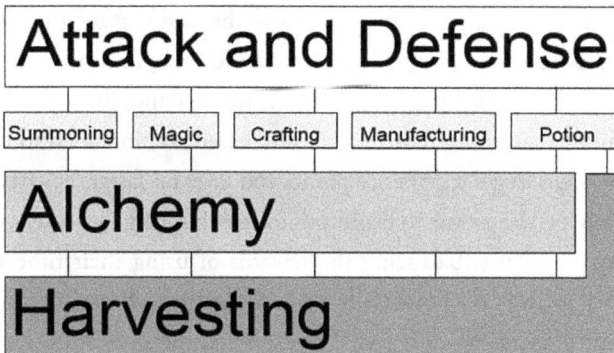

Figure 1.1 How EL's different skills are connected

EL used an "experience point" system in exactly the same way as every other online game. Every action related to a skill would earn experience points for that specific skill. For example, producing magic essences

---

[1]Special thanks to Mark Holton for assisting with this graphic.

would earn alchemy experience. Each skill had its own separate count for experience points, and each level took more experience points than the previous level, so leveling up would naturally take longer as a player's level increased. The skill system in EL also included an "overall level" that added up the total experience points gained from every skill. And the difficulty scaled up with each level. For example, in manufacturing, reliably producing steel shields required a higher level than producing iron shields, while fighters could choose different level monsters to fight against.

It was a simple and effective design, but this was not obvious to new players, and the game did not provide any clues about how to play. This left the frustrated new players to rely on hunting small animals and selling the fur. The lucky ones, like me, were eventually introduced to the lilac bush, where they could pick their way out of poverty. The rest, like j_wag17, simply quit, because, without any guides, it took too long to learn how to play the game.

The Economics (Types of Goods)

Every player in EL was looking to maximize the usefulness of their time. In the game, this means trying to achieve the best combination of gold coins and experience points. Gold coins could buy products, and experience points would lead to higher levels. It was a reinforcing dynamic, because almost everything that a player purchased was intended to make it easier for them to get experience points and level up faster. For new players, the most obvious way to begin was to start hunting low-level animals, but every player was balancing the rewards of using their time against the risks of giving up a potentially more profitable option. In economics, this is called an *opportunity cost*. For example, the opportunity costs of choosing to hunt animals included other options such as the potential to be exploring the game instead (and find something like the lilac bush), or consider whether there was something more enjoyable outside the game. Everyone weighs these opportunities in their own way, and I decided to continue hunting while my brothers made other choices. None of those choices were exactly wrong or right, but they were measured individually on the basis of how each one of us valued our time.

Moving beyond small animals was difficult without knowing what to do next. There was a *barrier to entry* to moving farther in the game. A barrier to entry is a feature (such as startup costs or government regulations) that makes it difficult to enter a new market. In this case, it was the startup costs, counted in both money and knowledge. In the real world, some examples of industries with high startup costs that require lots of initial investments are oil production, railroads, and utilities. For the game, it was the fact that buying new weapons and armor was too expensive for a new player. They could not level up quickly without making that initial investment, and they could not get that initial investment without knowing where to find the money.

The lilac bush offered a fast way to earn gold coins, and it solved the new investment problem, but it also introduced some irregularities into the game world. The first is how it affected the problem of *scarcity*. Scarcity is the economic description of how we make decisions on the basis of a limited amount of resources and theoretically unlimited demands. Because the lilac bush would never run out of flowers, it was an unlimited resource, and the problem of scarcity shifts from limited resources to just limited time. The problem of unlimited flowers is compounded by the bottomless pockets of the NPC. By having an NPC that would buy lilacs (or any other potential item) without changing its price, the game was effectively setting a *price floor* on the price of lilacs that prevented the market from showing their true value. A price floor is a limit to how low a market price can go. It is effective only if the normal market price is lower than the price floor, and it's relatively easy to see that the price floor on lilacs was effective. With an unlimited amount of easy lilacs available, the price should be pretty close to zero. Who would want to pay for lilacs if everyone could get them for free? Only an NPC.[2]

This easy way of earning money made it possible for both fighters and producers to move on to more advanced ways of playing the game. For players who wanted to focus on production, it took months of harvesting before they could switch to manufacturing full time. This was because, as

---

[2]On the other side, an NPC could set a *price ceiling* by selling unlimited goods at a specific price, but these were not in effect for most of the items in the game, because the market prices were generally much lower than the price ceiling.

we'll see later, manufacturing was painfully unprofitable, and harvesting for money is how players made up the difference. For now, it is sufficient to see how this market worked. Figure 1.2 provides another look at the structure of the game skills, but now we can think of them as markets, rather than just skills.

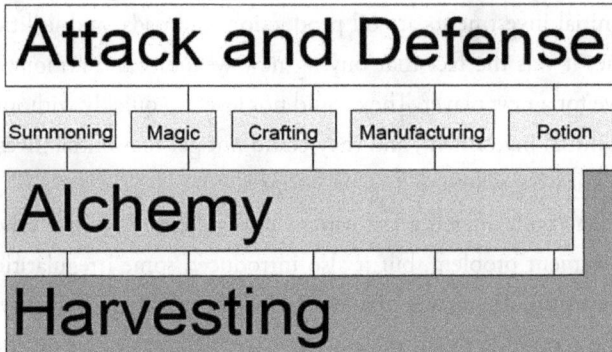

Figure 1.2 How EL's different markets are connected

Each step of the manufacturing production process transformed the product into a higher-stage product. In economics terms, every item represented a different step of the production cycle, and each skill generally produced one of three different types of goods: *raw materials, intermediate goods, or finished products.* Raw materials are the basic unprocessed materials that are used to make other goods. Intermediate goods are the processed raw materials that have been upgraded into something more useful for the next step of manufacturing. The end result of the manufacturing process is finished products, or finished goods, that are sold to their final customers. We can describe the process in EL by showing what types of products were produced at each step of the supply chain:

1. Harvest coal and iron ore (harvesting to get raw materials).
2. Make iron and steel bars (using alchemy to make intermediate goods).
3. Manufacture swords and armor (manufacturing to make finished products).
4. Sell manufactured items (selling finished products) to other players.

Table 1.1 should make it easier to understand what this means when it's applied to the game world and the real world.

Table 1.1 How EL's markets match real world markets

	Raw materials	Intermediate goods	Finished products
Game skill required	Harvesting	Alchemy	Manufacturing Crafting Potions
Game world products	Flowers, minerals, and metal ores	Magic essences and metal bars	Potions, weapons and armor, and special rings and medallions
Real world businesses	Farming, mining, and drilling	Milling, smelting, and refining	Manufacturing
Real world products	Grains, oil, coal, sand, and metal ores	Steel, glass, and aluminum	Almost anything you can buy at the store

The big idea is that, at a basic level, the game world of EL can be described using the exact same definitions that are used in the real world. From here, we can begin to discuss more advanced economic ideas.

CHAPTER 2

RIVA

I made pretty good money by working alone, at least by newbie standards. My production was not fast, but I could earn about 10,000 gold coins every week by selling swords and armor, and every batch raised my manufacturing skill by a few levels. It was a grind, but I enjoyed it. I played the game as if I was the only player in the game. I could make money selling manufactured items and use that money to train other skills. I chatted with other players, but I played alone. It was almost like a mining simulator with a chat room attached. I didn't think that I needed anyone else.

What changed my mind was a player who approached me while I was walking to the iron mines in the Desert Pines (DP). He asked if I would like to join his guild. A guild, in this game, was a group of players who formally associated with each other and played the game as a team. This player's guild was named SILK.

I told him that I didn't need a guild; I was doing just fine on my own. My brother, robo2917, had joined a guild a few weeks earlier, but they never seemed to do anything together, so I did not see a personal benefit. The player insisted that the game was much easier to play as part of a team. I was not fully convinced, but I decided to give it a try. I became a member of SILK.

SILK was considered a testing guild for another guild named RIVA. The point was that new players would be able to prove themselves in SILK and get promoted into RIVA. It was an unusual arrangement that no other guild used, but RIVA had a reputation to maintain and did not want to get it ruined by a reckless newbie. After about 3 months, the leadership of RIVA decided that it was better to combine the two guilds, and SILK merged with RIVA.[1] I went along with the plan.

---

[1]After the merger, RIVA became the game's second largest guild, with 80 members. The median guild at the time had about 10 members, while the largest had 116.

The more time I spent with RIVA, the more I understood the big picture of the social game above the individual players. Inside the rules set by Entropy and his moderators (the players who volunteered to enforce the rules), guilds appeared to operate as independent businesses or individual countries. Most guilds were established with a single leader called a guild master, and the guild master would be in charge of running the guild. A few guilds elected their guild master, but the game did not have a way to enforce voting. The only way for the leadership to change was if the guild master agreed to give up the position. (Which might not happen!)

The relationship between different guilds in Eternal Lands (EL) was an emotionally charged issue. Some guilds were more competitive than others, but each had its own focus. There were three main types of guilds: social guilds, economic guilds, and fighting guilds. But the two most important ones were the economic guilds and fighting guilds. Economics-based guilds, which usually called themselves manufacturers or merchants, focused on supplying fighters through manufacturing weapons and armor or crafting jewelry. The fighting guilds were the military powers of EL; there were no fighting quests in the game, so their strength was built on attacking other players and overpowering other fighting guilds. They often camped in the areas of the game that were marked for player killing. Player killing, known as "pk," is simply the act of killing another player (instead of killing a monster). Only specifically marked areas allowed pk, and anyone who went into a pk area could easily end up in the Underworld.[2] This was where the fighters went to war.

These two types of guilds did not compete with each other. Each guild had its own flavor and attracted a different type of player. The producing guilds wanted money and the military guilds needed weapons and armor, so they traded. It was just an expanded version of the role that individual players chose for themselves. Some were manufacturers and some were fighters.

Fighting guilds were almost always at war with each other, mostly for no reason at all, but the trading markets were mysteriously harmonious. Although the economics-based guilds actively competed with each

---

[2] Sometimes pk was modified to say "pked" or "pking" just like any other action word.

other, they all believed that everyone had room to make money. Everyone had their own place in the market, and nobody had any fear of getting pushed out. RIVA was probably the most powerful manufacturer, and it had the ability to make the game difficult for other manufacturers, but RIVA chose not to try, because the guild wanted to keep a good reputation.

RIVA was a well-established guild of manufacturers who produced and traded swords, armors, potions, rings, and any other conceivably profitable item. The only thing that RIVA asked from its members was that they give some of their time helping the guild make money. The guild needed people to harvest for them, and the guild members who gave enough of their time would be promoted to a higher guild rank.

RIVA's leaders sent me to the White Stone (WS) mines, the DP mines, and the other mines around the game world. I harvested their flowers and their coal. I walked around the world to get their supplies, and brought them all back to RIVA's home base, a storage space in the middle of the massive WS forest. And while I walked and talked with RIVA's members, the guild introduced me to a new way of playing the game.

Before I joined the guild, I thought of EL as a single-player game with a chat room attached. Other players were around, but I worked alone. I did all of my own harvesting, all of my own alchemy, and all of my own manufacturing. I avoided other players as much as possible, and only dealt with them when I had something to sell. RIVA's methods were different. The guild would harvest as a group, pool the resources, and then choose a high-ranking member to manufacture swords and armor. It was fast and efficient, and it made RIVA a powerful manufacturer.[3]

Being part of a guild also meant that people recognized me as part of a guild. The game showed every player's name above their head, and to the right of their name was a four letter guild designation called a guild tag. Other players would see this tag and instantly have a clue about my reputation. I was part of RIVA, and RIVA was an honorable guild, so I must be an honorable person.

---

[3]RIVA could have used this power to push others out of the market, but RIVA did not play that way. RIVA's goal was to be honorable and friendly, not to be competitive.

The Economics (Inputs and Outputs)

From a market perspective, the manufacturing guilds were the producers/ suppliers and the fighting guilds were the consumers. If we follow this into the economic theory, each market has a balance between what people are willing to sell (*supply*) and what people are willing to buy (*demand*). Where these two sides match up is what determines the market price. When the supply, demand, and price all agree, it's called the *market equilibrium*. When supply or demand changes, the price changes, and so does the equilibrium. In the coming chapters we'll see how this interaction works, but for now it's enough to know that this is how the two sides of the market worked in EL, and it affected the way that some guilds conducted their business.

Every manufacturing guild had to decide what to produce. In real world economics, this means looking at how a company uses *inputs* (what you put in) to get *outputs* (what you get out, or the finished products), and this is based on the four major inputs: *land, labor, capital,* and *entrepreneurship*. Land includes the land and natural resources. Labor is the people who work for the company. Capital is the equipment used for production.[4] And entrepreneurship is the managers who bring it all together. The production for EL included all four of these factors:

- Land in EL is the flowers, coal, and metal ore that players could harvest.
- Labor is the players who worked for the guild.
- Capital is the equipment that the players used, such as pickaxes for harvesting.
- Entrepreneurship is the leadership of the guild who made the decisions about what to produce and sell.

For almost every guild, these factors were all very similar. They all had access to the same land and equipment, and most of them had similar quality workers and leadership. This is because almost everyone used the same method of production. Every individual player would harvest their own materials, do their own manufacturing, and sell their own items.

---

[4]There are different types of capital, but, for simplicity, we are limiting this description to equipment or tools used for production.

They were officially guilds, but they were not taking advantage of the benefits from using teamwork. RIVA was different. RIVA used its workers in a better way.

RIVA operated in a way that was different from every other guild in the game. Other guilds had each player do every step of the production process on their own. RIVA chose to have each player specialize in one step of the process. To see what this means, let's go back to the steps from the last chapter. For every other guild, and every player outside a guild, these steps were taken one at a time.

1. Harvest coal and iron ore (harvesting as an individual).
2. Make iron and steel bars (using alchemy as an individual).
3. Manufacture swords and armor (manufacturing as an individual).
4. Sell manufactured items to other players (selling as an individual).

RIVA made a small change with a big effect.

1. Harvest coal and iron ore (harvesting *as a group*).
2. Make iron and steel bars (using alchemy *as a group*).
3. *Combine the resources.*
4. Manufacture swords and armor (one manufacturing specialist for the group).
5. Sell manufactured items to other players (one selling specialist for the group).
6. Split the rewards.

This method gave RIVA an advantage called *economies of scale*. What this means is that, as the size of the operation grew larger, it became cheaper for the guild to produce. For RIVA, this led to lower costs and higher profits. The players within RIVA used their time more efficiently because they didn't have to take the time switching from one skill to another, and the guild could build up its resources faster than each player doing every step all alone. Every RIVA guild member could specialize in one task.

A good real world comparison is Henry Ford's famous assembly lines. Henry Ford was not the first to use an assembly line—Adam Smith describes the idea as a design of a pin factory in his book, *The Wealth of Nations*, from 1776—but his innovation transformed the automobile industry. Each worker specialized in a very specific task and became an expert at one part of production. This made it faster to produce, cutting the time to build a car from 12 hours to 2.5 hours, because the workers did not lose any time switching tasks and they became more skilled at their one task (History.com 2009; Tedlow 2001). It was also easier to train a worker to do only one thing.

RIVA could have been the Ford Motor Company of EL. RIVA's method of production was much faster and more efficient, and it gave the guild an obvious advantage in the marketplace. Other guilds were close to the same size, but they didn't use their labor in an efficient way, so RIVA was effectively giving itself cheaper labor. RIVA's unique way of manufacturing also showed an advantage in leadership over other guilds, and the guild was well managed.

RIVA could have seized its advantage, but RIVA's potential market power was limited by its desire to play in an honorable way. The guild had an incredible amount of what is called *reputational capital*. Reputational capital is the value and goodwill that comes from being known as an ethical or a trustworthy organization or person. It takes a long time to build and only minutes to destroy. This capital can even go negative. This was part of the game that almost everyone cared about; even fighting guilds had an informal honor code. If RIVA used its potential market power to push around the other players, it would be sacrificing some of its reputational capital, and possibly jeopardizing some of its sales.

In the business world, reputational capital is essential for companies that need to sell safe products to their customers. A powerful example of the importance of reputational capital is Chipotle. The company saw a massive decline in sales after hundreds of people became sick with *E. coli* infections from eating Chipotle products (Little 2016). Chipotle did eventually begin to recover, but it took a few years. Other industries, such as banking, oil and gas, and telecommunications, tend to be less concerned about reputational capital, because it's harder for their customers to switch to a competitor.[5] The harder it is for customers to switch to another service, the less a business will have to care about how their customers actually feel about their service.

---

[5] My friends in the banking industry insist that not every bank behaves this way, but the incentive for large banks is real.

PART II
A New Guild

CHAPTER 3

RICH Is Born

While I worked as an anonymous low-level piece of one of the game's most powerful guilds, my brother, robo2917, moved from guild to guild as he looked for an easy opportunity to become a high-level guild leader. He eventually found a guild that would allow him to advance by paying the guild master. It was a simple idea: Harvest lilacs, collect money, and give money to the guild master. But it didn't take long for him to see that this arrangement was meant to make his guild master rich. He could advance, but the price was more than just too much money, because he was also paying with his dignity. It was not worth it. This led my brother to decide that he should have his own guild. Then *he* could be the one collecting money, and *he* would be the one getting rich! But he needed my help.

To make a guild, the game required 30,000 gold coins and at least one skill above level 38. My brother had the money, but he didn't have the skills. My harvesting skill was above 38, so I could create the guild for him if he gave me the money. But I actually liked RIVA, and I was a little reluctant to leave. On the other hand, when I thought about it, I realized that RIVA was using my time in the same way that my brother's guild was taking his money: They promised promotions for anyone who contributed to the guild's projects, but the price to advance was nearly impossible to pay. I would never be one of RIVA's guild leaders. The line for those positions was just too long. And even though I didn't really want to be a guild leader, I thought it was unfair for RIVA to overlook its low-level guild members. Promotions should not be based on who can pay the most.

So I made my choice. I sent a message to RIVA's guild master. I said that I was leaving to help my brother start his own guild, but I would be back if it failed. He was skeptical but supportive. He probably knew that I had no plan to come back.

To get our new guild started, the first thing we had to do was come up with a name. Guild names can be long, but the guild tags can only be four letters, so most guilds chose a name that fit an attractive acronym. We did not want to make an acronym. We just wanted a name. And there were many four-letter words we could have chosen, but there's only one that could accurately describe our goals. We decided to call ourselves RICH, because we knew that we would become rich. robo2917 would be the guild master, and I would be his number two.

It was surprisingly easy. robo2917 gave me the 30,000 gold coins, I punched in the code to make a new guild—*#create_guild RICH*—and everything was ready. Well, almost. A few minutes after RICH was first created, the game's server crashed.

The crash erased the guild and destroyed our money. No problem. I had more than enough swords to make another 30,000 gold coins. We could try it again.

I stood at the market in the Valley of the Dwarves (VOTD) and connected to the market channel, where I announced that I was selling swords at the game's market prices. At first the sales were fast. Buyers came in from all over the game world. Then, after I made a few thousand gold coins, the buying stopped. I didn't have the patience to wait for more buyers to show up, and I needed to get my money fast, so I tried again. This time, I advertised my swords as quality premium swords, and tried to use the same market prices. Still no buyers. So I tried again, emphasizing that my swords were the best swords a player could buy, but no one was interested. Anyone who wanted a sword at that price was already satisfied. I had to try something different.

I knew that my swords were the same as everyone else's swords, and I recognized that it was not possible to fool the buyers into thinking there was a difference; the only way I could offer something better was to lower my price. I went back to the market channel with a much better offer, announcing swords on sale at extra low prices. I cut the price of my swords to 50 gold coins lower than the established market prices. It was a significant discount.

It worked. The buyers returned, until, again, they were satisfied.

So I made an even better offer: The same swords at an even lower price! And again, the buyers returned, until they too were satisfied. The cycle continued until I sold every sword in my inventory. It was a fascinating discovery. When I sold my swords, I realized that the fastest way to sell things in the game was to keep lowering the price. This idea, that lowering the prices will sell more swords, would later become the basis for everything that I did in Eternal Lands (EL). And it only came from the need to make the guild again.

Using the money that I made from selling my swords, I created the guild again. Then the server crashed for a second time, this time taking the guild, my money, and my swords. It was almost everything we owned.

Now we were broke. We still didn't have a guild, and it would take days to make another 30,000 gold coins. The only reason we could try a third time (and this time it worked) is because one of my brother's old guilds offered to donate the money that we needed. I can't remember their name, but I never forgot their generosity.

The Economics (Perfect Competition)

What I had discovered, without knowing it, was a fundamental rule of economics. What I stumbled on while selling my swords is a concept called the *law of demand.* The more I lowered my price, the more swords I could sell. If I took a survey of the prices that a player was willing to pay, then I would have been able to build a model of their individual demand, and it would follow the same rule that I had discovered: *When the price goes down, the amount of product that people are willing to buy will go up.* For example, someone might buy twice as much if the price was cut in half. If I could somehow add up the demand for each individual, I could find the total market demand for a product at every price, but that was not necessary for finding the right price to sell. The only thing I needed to know was that people will buy more when the price goes down.

My failed attempt to call my swords premium swords was also an important introduction to the types of markets inside EL. I knew that my swords were not actually any better than anyone else's swords, but it was worth trying because I would make more money if it worked. It did not work, but it was still a valuable experiment because it confirmed that the EL markets were based on price. No one would be able to gain an advantage by advertising higher quality because everyone had the same quality, and anyone selling below the market price would be bought out of the market. This type of market is called a *perfectly competitive market*. A perfectly competitive market is one with a large number of buyers and sellers who all sell exactly the same product, and none of them are big enough to influence the price in any meaningful way. For EL, if we disregard RIVA, a guild with the potential for market power that did not seek competition, this is a perfect description of its market. In the real world, the most commonly cited example of a perfectly competitive market is the market for grain: There are a huge number of farmers who all sell an identical product, and they must take whatever price the market offers. Any advantages are temporary and quickly copied by competitors or snuffed out by market forces.

CHAPTER 4

The Dying Ember

We advertised RICH as a guild for players who wanted to become rich. robo2917 walked around the game world wearing a full set of iron plate armor, the most expensive armor in the game, while I used him as an example of what new players could become if they joined the guild. Our plan was to try to get as many guild members as possible, and then use our number of members as a selling point for gaining even more members. We didn't actually have anything for them to do. Our purpose was to provide an environment where every player was accepted as an important part of the guild; we did not care if someone had a low level, and we did not care if other guilds rejected them. We were willing to take anyone and give them a chance to be part of RICH.

And we did. We took anyone who was willing to join us. It made the guild grow faster than other guilds in the game, but it also meant that we were taking reckless risks with our reputation. Our recruiting methods attracted the worst kind of player, especially the ones that other guilds had a good reason to avoid. And our rules allowed them to terrorize other players. We allowed, and sometimes encouraged, pking and mugging other players, looting and robbery, being rude, and otherwise violating the social standards of Eternal Lands (EL). By accepting the players that no other guild wanted to take, RICH established a culture of outsiders who were willing to experiment with new ways of playing the game. But there was not enough discipline in the RICH guild's leadership to prevent it from slipping into a bad reputation.

The RICH guild's beginning was as shaky as the EL server. My brother and I had absolutely no idea about how to run a successful guild. I only wanted to play as a manufacturer; my preference was to stay behind the scenes, making items to make money, and I would continue to do this on my own. My brother wanted to be a fighter. The difference in our styles was an informal split within the guild. RICH was trying to become both a merchant guild and a fighting guild at the same time. It was an organizational structure without a design or an identity. Players got promoted if my brother wanted them to be promoted (which usually meant that they paid him), and we never tried to see if they were actually good leaders. It was chaotic, but entertaining.

None of this was impossible to repair. RICH was still a relatively invisible guild, with about 60 total members and no established reputation, and people were usually willing to give new guilds a chance to earn their reputation. Whenever there was a problem, the RICH guild was usually forgiven, and the RICH member's attitude did not count against it. But an entire guild cannot be rude forever and expect to remain invisible. With enough time and enough complaints, a bad reputation would inevitably stick.

When RICH was only a few months old, one of the members reported something that I had never seen before. Walking around the game was a player with a bright red name. This was exciting for the RICH guild's fighters, because, in EL, a bright red name is the signal of an outlaw punished for breaking EL rules. Attacking other players was only possible in places marked for pk. But a player with a red name could be attacked anywhere. This meant that the red name was an invitation to attack them anywhere in the game. RICH had an opportunity to hunt a criminal. RICH could be part of their punishment and earn an instant reputation as a group of good guys who kill the bad guys.

RICH was not the first to kill the red name, but RICH was ready for their death. Because every player who dies ends up in the Underworld, and the exit from the Underworld leads to a lamppost in Isla Prima, RICH camped by the lamppost and waited. And when the red name player finally appeared, the RICH guild players killed it. When it came back to the lamppost, RICH killed it again, and when it came back again, RICH killed it again.

RICH kept attacking the helpless red name player until it began to beg for mercy. Most of the guild stopped at mercy, but some continued; it was not against the guild's rules, and each kill was rewarded with more of the player's valuable items. The fighters were butchering a helpless player

THE DYING EMBER 27

begging for mercy, but the player they were attacking was an outlaw, and the items this player dropped were making them rich. Over the course of a few hours, RICH players captured about 15,000 gold coins worth of items just from killing the red name player. It was a windfall that I could not compel the guild to return.

The red name player spent half a day in the Underworld before RICH finally got bored. Nobody knew what the player had done to earn a red name, but that was not important. The moderators—the game's volunteer police force, judge, and jury—chose to give this player a red name, and we were just part of the punishment. We were taking justice to an outlaw.

But we were wrong.

The red name player was not an outlaw. The player that RICH condemned to the Underworld was actually a popular moderator named Ember. She was only testing the red name punishment. And RICH had just proven, in the most scandalous way possible, that it was a *very* effective punishment. This time, it was not about attacking a nobody for no reason; it was about murdering someone who served as part of EL's virtual police force.

Later that night, Ember put her story of the RICH guild's behavior in the guilds and clans section of the official EL forums.[1] Ember's complaint, posted on March 28, 2005, described a dishonorable guild of bandits who could not be trusted to keep their promises. robo2917 had made a deal with her. RICH promised to leave her alone, but the guild continued to kill her for hours after he said that they would stop. From her perspective, robo2917's promise was empty.

"hEaL Members and allies," she announced, "**I am asking for your help.** I would like a ban on the Rich guild." What Ember called for was extreme: no trading, no helping, no pleasant conversation. She asked that the other guilds in EL look at RICH as a group of outlaws and pk them on sight (Ember 2005). The responses came in fast.

---

[1] The official EL forums were a public message board managed by Entropy and the game's moderators where players went to talk about the politics and economics of the game. It is the primary source for almost all of the disputes that appear in this book.

i agree RICH is a horrible newb guild my guild will join your ban-
ning of them. (valo13 2005)

Twin will not help RICH. (Kala 2005)

We'll put them on our PK lists too. Only the biggest jerks make
Ember's guild's PK list it seems. (Daxon 2005)

One player already had experience with RICH. "i can def assure u
that these guys deserve it. ... Most of them are scammin lien and kinda
dumb, and they are very rude to everyone." (valo13 2005). When other
players asked him for an explanation, he continued with a summary:

i'll give u a few of my reasons, first a very crappy attempt at a scam,
2nd tried to send a spy, 3rd they constantly run their mouths off
to everyone yet wont step foot into pk unless its empty. If it was
just 1 or 2 members it would be different, but nearly the whole
guild acts the same way. (valo13 2005)

This was all true. RICH members had also attempted to scam, spy
on, and steal from other guilds. The RICH guild's separate individual
offenses were spilled out in one big public topic. The RICH reputation
was cemented.

seanodonnell, an Irish programmer in his late 20s, was the only RICH
member to come to the guild's defense. "I know Rich is a good guild with
good people," he said in the forums. "I would be very interested to talk
to anyone who can tell me how RICH has suddenly obtained such a bad
name." (seanodonnell 2005).

He posted again only a few hours later.

Well I have been talking with ember, mind and robo to try and
figure out what has been going on. Mind and Robo ... have asked
me to apologize on their behalf for pking Ember. They found
her pkable on a non pk map, and initially assumed that she must
therefore want to fight, but things got carried away and she was
repeatedly pked after it was clear this was not the case. Arrange-
ments are being made to return/replace any items Ember dropped.
... Apologies again to Ember. (seanodonnell 2005)

His diplomatic efforts, which I eventually joined, were countered by more accusations and insults. It did not matter what we said or how sincerely we apologized for the misunderstanding. Even when Ember's direct recording of the incident showed me kicking players out of the guild for not returning her items and asking her why she was pkable, the other guilds still took her side. By attacking and harassing a moderator, RICH broke one of the game's most sacred unofficial rules, and most guilds (except RIVA, the game's only truly neutral guild), agreed to support the ban.

While the conversation in the EL forums raged on, the guild began to collapse. The heated spotlight prompted me to start ferociously booting the guild's worst offenders, while many of the best RICH members, effectively locked out of the game's social world, abandoned the guild. The RICH guild's membership dropped from over 60 total members to less than 10 active players. And with the remaining players questioning the purpose of the guild, I became concerned that RICH might not survive. To stop the chaos, I quietly signed in to robo2917's player account and stole the guild master title from my brother. I told him that he could stay, but he decided to leave on his own.[2]

In the days that followed, the social pressure proved surprisingly effective. A RICH tag was a signal for harassment, and the guild continued to struggle. I was not sure what to do, but I didn't think that I should be the one controlling RICH. The reality was that running a good guild was beyond my ability, and the guild's collapse was just as much my fault as it was my brother's. I had no interest in becoming the guild master, and I did not take over just to take over. I took over to give it away to someone older.

The most qualified person to run the guild, by far, was seanodonnell. He was not part of the red name slaughter, and his efforts to defend my leadership were more than the guild deserved. I thought that he would be a better guild master than me, so I offered him the job.

He said no. The guild was not his guild, and I would have to be the one to decide what to do next.

---

[2]My brother was justifiably upset by my betrayal, and he paid me back later by causing me to get temporarily banned from the game, but we're still on the same team. This is the kind of thing that only a brother can forgive.

I asked the remaining guild members if we should change the name of our guild to try and reset our reputation.

It was unanimous—*no*. Everyone who stayed with RICH wanted to be part of RICH, and they all preferred the RICH name.

I had limited options. I did not want to be the leader, but neither did anyone else. Anyone with a RICH label would always be a dishonorable outsider, and it was nearly impossible to play the game with such a toxic guild tag. This left me with two options: I could give up and destroy the guild myself, or I could make it something new. But if I wanted to keep the guild alive, then I would have to be the face of it, and I would have to own the reputation that it earned.

It became an easy decision. What RICH represented was an opportunity to try something totally new. I would attempt to repair the guild's reputation, but if that proved to be impossible, then there would be no incentive to apologize. If EL could only see RICH as evil, then that's the part I would play and that's the character I would become.

The Economics (Reputational Capital)

I learned it the hard way. Even with an honest mistake, reputational capital can be erased within a day. An unpleasant accusation alone can be enough to flip an outsider's opinion, especially when the accusation comes from a source that appears to be trustworthy. My experience ultimately showed that regaining a neutral reputation takes more effort than building a positive one. When a reputation is already negative, there's a resistance to moving positive, and the more negative, the more resistance. I was not looking to become an outlaw, but the longer other players disregarded my attempts to make peace, the more attractive it was to play in a malicious way.

On the other hand, the boycott against RICH was surprisingly effective. The purpose of a boycott is to encourage an organization or a person to change their behavior. For that purpose, it worked. RICH began removing players who could not match the social expectations for the rest of the game, and it almost killed the guild. The reason the boycott was so successful was because it was comprehensive and widespread. It covered everything from refusing to buy RICH goods to callously avoiding and mocking RICH members. And almost everyone participated, because it was easy for players in EL markets to switch suppliers. RICH was unable to recover quickly. Potential new members knew what would happen if they joined, and they could see that *any other guild* was more attractive. The ones who stayed with RICH were not worried about what the outside world thought of the guild. As long as they believed that RICH was "a good guild with good people," they would stay and support what they thought was right.

In the real world, boycotts rarely result in meaningful changes. They are difficult to organize and enforce, because most people don't like to change their habits, and not everyone will agree with a boycott. They are also, in general, too broadly applied, and it is nearly impossible to boycott every product from a major corporation. Because of these features, boycotts do not have much of an effect on the profits or stock performance of a large company. For example, the Chick-fil-A boycott in 2012 did not have a significant impact on the company's sales. A smaller company, however, is likely to be much more negatively affected (Dubner 2016).

What boycotts can do, when they are focused, is affect a company's reputation and public commitment to social causes. They can also cause potential employees to think twice about joining. A great example of this effect is Monsanto, a company with such a toxic reputation that its name was discontinued after the company was acquired by Bayer. Consistent calls to boycott Monsanto products, whether justified or not, colored the company's reputation in such a way that potential employees could become uneasy about joining the company. Those employees would have justifiable concerns about associating with Monsanto. This is the same effect that we saw with RICH (Dubner 2016; Brodwin 2018).

CHAPTER 5

Join Guild RICH

After a few weeks of honest efforts to make peace with Ember, her guild abandoned her. She was holding on to a hatred that the rest of her guild no longer shared, and they decided to leave. Her guild dissolved and she stepped down from her moderator position. The other guilds that supported the boycott allowed RICH to trade again. The stained reputation lingered, but the original reason for the trading ban was forgotten.

Inside the guild, I was able to convince the last few members to stick around. After the pk disaster that nearly crushed the guild, I decided that the RICH guild should never become involved with any more fighting. Even if I was looking to start a war, RICH would not win. I kicked out most of the guild's fighters, and no one was willing to supply RICH with weapons and armor for fighting. Fighting with other players (and a long list of other problematic behavior) was now officially against the guild rules. Anyone who wanted to fight a military war was no longer accepted as a member of RICH.

Getting cut off from the rest of Eternal Lands (EL) had also forced RICH to begin manufacturing its own items. No one would trade with the guild, and it made sense to become self-sufficient. I had no desire to make RICH a military power, and without anyone pushing for that type of gameplay, operating as an economic guild would be much easier. I began to imagine what the guild could become. When I thought about my experience with RIVA, which was watching a large guild coordinate many different pieces to produce a large number of items, and combined that with the RICH guild's reputation, I saw something that nobody else in EL could see. RIVA was the only guild in the game with any real manufacturing advantage, and it was handicapped by its desire to be seen as an honorable guild. But what if there was a guild with a reputation so low that it had nothing to lose? That guild could do what RIVA was doing without any concern for the social consequences.

I wanted RICH to be the *new* RIVA—a guild smart enough to influence the market but also bold enough to try it. RICH was not restricted by trying to play in an honorable way. Its reputation inside the game had become so negative that even an honest attempt to change was disregarded as a trick to fool people into trusting it. And beyond the bad reputation, RICH was also seen as powerless, like a small swarm of mosquitos that take a few bites but never do any real damage. So nobody backed RICH and nobody feared RICH. This meant that nobody would consider the guild to be a serious threat until it was already too late for them to compete with a new strategy.

My plan was to shamelessly copy RIVA's ideas. I would do almost everything that RIVA was already doing, but with a few minor adaptations. The first was that nobody would ever be required to work for me. I wanted to play with players who *wanted* to be RICH; promotions would be based on who provided the best ideas, not who paid me the most. This meant finding ways to persuade other players to harvest for me, even if I somehow had to pay them for it. The other difference was that I would not look for high profits. To be like RIVA and achieve lower costs was a good start, but I would take those lower costs and pass them on to my customers as lower prices.

I had no idea how I would do that, or what would happen, or how I would pay my workers, but I knew that I needed to try something big. It was not good enough just to build up to something respectable, because there was no real consequence for failure, and, as a high school student with extra free time, there was no limitation on how long I played the game. But to be big, I had to start with a big idea. At the time, the largest projects for most guilds never tried to reach above 10,000 fire essences (the basic element used to produce almost everything else). From there, they would slowly use up the essences while they sold weapons and armor. It was a smart way of managing sales, but, even if RICH used my new methods, 10,000 fire essences would not be enough get the guild excited. I needed something more. With that idea in my mind, I decided to shoot for a goal that no other guild could even imagine: RICH would produce

100,000 fire essences. No one would see that coming, and no one would be able to stop the flood when it finally came.

To complete such a large project, the guild needed more workers, preferably low-level players. To get these workers, I first had to convince them that RICH was the best guild for their goals. Then I had to convince them that this project was worth following. Fortunately, for both of these challenges, the game's design was on my side.

In EL, every item gave experience points the moment it was produced, and the player who made the item could choose to collect gold coins by selling it. In the case of fire essences, their per unit value (3.5 gold coins each) and experience (6 experience points each) were so low that only new players focused on making them, and players rarely sold them because they were more valuable when used for making higher-level items. This meant that they had value as a source of experience for a low-level player, but low-level players could not do anything with fire essences. On the other side, high-level players did not need such a small amount of experience, but they needed the fire essences to produce their high-level items. I saw a possibility for both sides to benefit. Maybe there was a way for the two sides to trade.

Making fire essences was also very slow. First, players had to walk to the Valley of the Dwarves (VOTD) to collect the flowers. Then they had to trek across the continent to harvest sulfur from the mines in the Desert Pines (DP), each time stopping at a storage that could be as far as a 10-minute round-trip. It was simple, but it wasn't easy. Every character had a limit on how much they could carry, and most new players were unable to carry more than 200 flowers or 100 sulfur at a time. Each fire essence required two flowers and one sulfur, so reaching my goal of 100,000 fire essences meant collecting 200,000 flowers and 100,000 sulfur. This was impossible for a single player to do all alone. But with 10 players, or 20, or 30, all working together, it could be done within a few days. That was my plan.

RICH was already building an army of noobs (new players with no experience inside EL were known as "noobs" in the game). From the time that my brother and I started the guild, we knew that RICH would be a guild that gives everyone a chance no matter how long they've been playing the game. And although I became more selective with my recruiting and stricter with my rules, this proved to be the right idea. RICH continued to seek out the players that nobody wanted to take. No other guild in the game recruited low-level players, and this allowed me to focus on adding new members without competing against other guilds. Other guilds could have specific requirements about what skills their new members needed, but RICH did not care about that. Other guilds wanted players with EL game experience, but RICH just wanted smart players, players who were willing to learn the RICH way of playing (and hopefully willing to harvest flowers for me).

I no longer used my brother's flashy high-end style to attract new members. The new RICH leadership adopted a more hardworking appeal. It was the kind of look that says they're always in the mines. I emphasized my own style, wearing a brown harvester's cape and a brown fur hat, often carrying a pickaxe. I thought it would show a leader who sees himself on the same level as everyone else in the guild. Being RICH was not about looking rich. Being RICH was about being willing to walk into the mines and try to build something incredible. And anytime RICH went into the mines, I would be standing there too, with my pickaxe, harvesting with everyone else.

I walked around the game world asking everyone I saw, "Would you like to join the RICH guild?" If they didn't already have a guild, then they were a potential RICH member. Almost everyone immediately agreed, but if they were not initially interested, then I would try to persuade them that RICH was the best guild in the game, and I would let them know that they could leave if they didn't like it. If they were still not interested, then I would ask them if they needed any help. Every new player who was not a new member was at least a potential future ally.

I was constantly selling the guild. I promoted RICH as the guild walked back and forth from the DP mines to the DP storage. I sent messages to everyone who stood in the VOTD markets. Sometimes I paraded around Isla Prima (IP) handing out fur coats to new players and telling them about RICH. I even tried to catch the players who wanted to buy something from me. As one old member remembered, "[The] biggest thing I trusted you with was buying one steel shield, [and] if I remember correctly, I walked out of that exchange with TWO Steel Shields and a new guild." He later added, "You probably could have gotten away with selling me 5 Steel Shields."[1] I never stopped selling.

I also followed the economic debates that took place inside the EL forums, where I kept note of which players could understand my philosophy. The most thoughtful, in my opinion, was trollson, an experienced rocket engineer in his late 30s. He outlined, many times, the data behind what drives decisions in the market. He described, in clear, calm, and consistent terms, the influence of the game's design. He rarely took strong sides on an issue, but when he did, he had a compelling reason, and everyone respected his questions. I had to have trollson join my guild. But when I approached him, he said that he preferred to play the game alone. It was only a lengthy discussion on the benefits of playing as a team (as well as an emphasis on the fact that he could leave whenever he wanted) that persuaded him to join RICH. I immediately promoted him to a guild leadership position, and he never left.

The remarkable part about RICH taking in these new members was that the guild continued to have a terrible reputation. Other guilds were hostile to RICH, but these guilds were also ignoring inexperienced players. RICH was building a presence among the newbies that no other guild was even considering. And I was not just pretending to be a friend. I actually meant it. I asked every new member the same three questions: "How old are you? Where are you from? What do you do for a living?" *And I memorized their answers.* I showed them that I cared.

As the number of members expanded, recruiting became easier. RICH was everywhere, almost always in large groups, and the guild's social atmosphere became an attraction by itself—inexperienced players who saw RICH in the mines began asking if they could join. RICH was soaking up the size of an average guild, taking in about 12 new players, almost every week. By May 19, 2005, my recruiting efforts had propelled RICH to number two on the list of the game's largest guilds, at 115 members.

With all of these new members getting pulled into the guild, RICH was able to produce 100,000 fire essences, far more than any guild ever, in about 2 weeks. But the speed of this project was not just based on the number of new members pouring into the guild, it was also influenced by

---

[1]TheDesolator, personal communication, August 5, 2013.

the incentives that the game provided. The project was not supported by *requiring* new members to help, like most of RIVA's projects. The RICH project was made possible by *persuading* new members to help. This came from the power of experience points.

Every time a player created an item, they would receive experience points for leveling up. For most new players, the only thing that they could reliably produce was fire essences.[2] And because fire essences also gave the lowest amount of experience, most high-level players did not consider producing fire essences to be worthy of their time. On the other end, while the fire essences as a product were worthless to new players, the experience was valuable to them, especially if that experience came in the volume that RICH was able to produce. This made it possible for the new RICH members to make these items without expecting to get paid—all they wanted was the experience points. So the offer that RICH made to all of its new members was fair: "You provide us with your labor; we'll provide you with a fast way to level up; and we'll keep the money." None of the low-level players ever refused this offer.

The players outside the guild could not understand why RICH members were so eager to work for me. What these new members were doing for RICH was something that they could have done on their own. And then, instead of only earning experience points, they could get both the experience points and the money. What the people on the outside could not see was that these low-level players didn't need the gold coins. The experience was so valuable to them, and RICH helped it come so fast, that they were willing to cooperate in ways that would make it faster to level up. No one was fooled into joining; new players could understand the credibility of the RICH model without having to "unlearn" an old way of playing.

RICH also leveraged a natural bonus system built inside the game's design. Anyone making fire essences would have a one in 10,000 chance of making an enriched fire essence (a rare fire essence that was necessary

---

[2]Every production item had a recommended level for when it could be reliably produced. Higher-level items could still be attempted, but they would have a higher failure rate until the player's level caught up to the item's recommended production level. Fire essences were the lowest level.

JOIN GUILD RICH 39

to make high-end weapons and armor such as iron plate mail pieces). By allowing the members to keep their enriched fire essences, RICH could easily reward those who helped the most. Whenever a player was lucky enough to produce an enriched essence, the guild would offer to buy it from them at a fair price (roughly 5,000 to 7,000 gold coins, a lottery-winning amount of money for a new player). Everyone wanted to be part of this project.[3]

It was a win-win-win situation. The guild built its wealth while its most helpful members were rewarded with both extraordinary wealth and experience. And if everything continued to work as planned, then the RICH customers would also be rewarded with much lower prices. The losers would be every other merchant guild in the game.

The Economics (Monopolistic Competition)

Seeking out the new players in the game was not intended to be a strategic decision. My only goal was to add new members as fast as possible, and the easiest way to do that was to look where no one else was looking. Every other guild in the game wanted to be elite and honorable, but this meant that they were all competing with each other for the same potential group of guild members. RICH avoided this competition by selling itself to a set of players who were not elite. We can think of this as a type of market. Unlike the perfectly competitive market for weapons and armor, where every guild was offering the same quality items, guilds could distinguish themselves to potential members by offering a different experience. This is called *monopolistic competition*. A market with monopolistic competition is one with a large number of competitors offering similar products that can be differentiated. A good example of this type of market is restaurants, where consumers can choose between Mexican food, Chinese food, Italian food, American food, or any other of a wide variety, and they can choose which restaurant within each of these categories (these

---

[3]Wearing a special cape would increase the chances of producing an enriched essence to one in 1,000. The RICH members who wore this cape while producing fire essences for RICH became very wealthy very quickly. Selling one enriched fire essence earned more than enough money to buy the cape.

restaurants primarily compete with others of the same type). In EL, players could choose between a fighting guild and a merchant guild, and they could pick the one that they liked the best (and, like restaurants, these guilds primarily competed with others of the same type).

RICH was offering something that no one else could offer. RICH was not concerned about game skills. It was easy for new players to join, and it was the fastest way for them to level up. Experience points were more valuable for new players than for high-level players, which created a stronger incentive to produce low-level products. The other side to this description is that high-level players put more value on their time, just like high-income people put more value on their time. Allowing RICH members to keep their enriched fire essences also introduced a type of lottery system—the most helpful players were the most likely to win an enriched fire essence.

It was cooperation in a competitive way, and each side was satisfied with what they traded to each other. Low-level players exchanged their time for experience points and a chance for a big payout. This is the core of economics: People make choices on the basis of their own limitations, and they have to compare what they're getting with what they're giving up. In other words, everyone evaluates their options within their *constraints* (limitations), and a *cost–benefit analysis* helps them decide if the benefits are worth the costs. The costs include *explicit costs* (what is paid) and *implicit costs* (hidden costs that are not directly measured).[4] As long as RICH could provide benefits that would cover the cost of the player's time and also be better than what other guilds offered, then RICH would continue to be their preferred choice.

Another part of the advantage that RICH was building came from an unintended focus on what is called *human capital*. Human capital is the quality of a person's skills, experience, and knowledge. It's the idea that a highly skilled, experienced, and knowledgeable worker is more valuable than an average worker. And RICH had a culture of encouraging players to be smart about playing the game. This culture was reinforced by emphasizing promotion based on ability. The players who could come up

---

[4]The broader term of *opportunity costs* (the best alternative opportunity that's given up) includes both explicit costs and implicit costs.

with the best ideas were the ones that I wanted to be part of the guild's leadership. Restated in terms of economics, RICH was accepting players who were perceived to have low human capital and investing in their improvement. RICH was also targeting human capital in a way that would make the guild smarter. No other guild was looking for smart players.

In the real world, just like in the game, human capital is an extremely valuable investment. Human capital is enhanced by education. For an individual person, this means going to school, trying new things, or reading a book. Anything that helps someone become smarter will help them in the future, even if what they learn is not useful right away. But everyone benefits when other people are also encouraged to go to school, try new things, or read a book. Supporting other people's education makes life better, easier, and safer. It just takes time for the results to show.[5]

For RICH, building human capital and rewarding new players had an impressive effect on the guild's production. The short version is that, if you think about the factors of production—land, labor, capital, and entrepreneurship—RICH was able to come up with a way to get the cheapest labor in the game while also attracting the highest quality of entrepreneurship. The game's design was paying RICH players in experience points, and RICH was collecting every other benefit. No one would be able to compete with it unless they copied it. But as long as RICH sucked in most of the game's new players, this plan would be almost impossible to copy, because other guilds would not have enough low-level players willing to work for experience.

---

[5] The economic idea behind this is a concept called *positive externalities*. It describes a situation where an investment in one area leads to benefits somewhere else. Since the organization making the investment does not directly see all of the benefits, they do not invest as much as they should. This leads to underinvestment in areas that produce positive externalities, such as education, health care, and infrastructure. The opposite of positive externalities is *negative externalities*. Negative externalities work in the other direction. This concept describes a situation where the costs from one market are paid somewhere else. It leads to too much investment in markets that cause pollution (or other negatives). Cleaning up the pollution is paid for by other markets, when it should be part of the original cost.

PART III
The Rise of RICH

CHAPTER 6

Market War I

Outside of the huge manufacturing project that was still in progress, RICH was still a small operation. But whenever RICH entered the market and announced better prices, anyone trying to sell at the "real" market price would lose out on a deal. For some players, this "undercutting" strategy was even more offensive than what RICH had done to Ember. Market competition was unacceptable in the eyes of the RICH competitors. *No one* played the game this way. The point of a merchant guild in Eternal Lands (EL) was to make stuff and sell stuff. There was enough room for everyone to make money, and anyone disrupting the equilibrium, even temporarily, was automatically labeled as a dangerous outsider. If someone offered lower prices, and those prices began to stick as the real market prices, then it would threaten the stability of the game's entire economy. If RICH had the potential to cause this kind of damage, even if it was (for now) considered a smaller guild, then it was easy for some players to see RICH as a threat to their way of doing business.

Even with a small manufacturing system, RICH could still annoy the bigger players. The first evidence of RICH influence came from a manufacturers' movement that started in the EL forums on June 4, 2005. It was headed by LochnessLobster, EL's highest-level manufacturer. He called it a manufacturers' strike.

He didn't provide many detailed reasons for the strike, but it was likely inspired by recent posts about an "Alchemist's Union" that was created with the goal of raising prices for alchemy products. Alchemy was a marginally profitable skill, but the manufacturers were only breaking even. If they could find a way to raise the prices for their weapons and armor, as the Alchemist's Union had claimed to do for alchemy, then they would have more money and power in the game.

"We have power united," he declared, and the other manufacturers agreed (LochnessLobster 2005). They all faced the same problem. No one who focused on manufacturing could make any money, so they came to a resolution: They would go on strike and stay out of the market until prices rose, and when they came back to the market, they would fix the prices for weapons and armor. If their plan worked, then they would achieve their goal of raising the prices and eventually raise their profits. If their plan did not work, then they would be in the same position that they were before the strike—they would be harvesting lilacs to earn money and manufacturing to level up.

The idea was popular among the high-level manufacturers. But the fighters who bought their weapons and armor—the manufacturers' customers—were concerned that they were about to get taken advantage of. They paid prices that they thought were fair, and they were not going to pay more just to help someone else make money. They would buy from whoever listed the best price, and they didn't care how that person made their items or who that person was associated with. What mattered was the price.

I did not support the market strike. But, as a curious outside observer, I acknowledged that "Getting the stuff off of the market is a good way to raise the prices," and I decided to pull RICH out of the market to see what would happen (Mr.Mind 2005). Other manufacturers did the same, and the market channel fell nearly silent. Buyers hunting for deals were the only voices left, but they were not finding much to buy.

As the strike dragged on, stretching into days, buyers began to bid up what was left in the market. Prices rose modestly, and the strikers were satisfied to see their efforts making progress. *But they weren't making any money!* The players who joined the strike succeeded in raising the prices, but the only people making money were the ones who stayed in the market. From my perspective, achieving their official goal of raising prices was also making it impossible for the market strikers to reach their unofficial goal of making high profits. After watching the effects of the strike for about a week, with prices for some items nearly 50 percent higher than before, I decided that it was time for me to capture some of the profits. I stepped into the market to sell some high-end iron plate mail armor.

I made an incredible amount of money, about 50,000 gold coins, within a few minutes, before LochnessLobster saw what I was doing. "The strike is broken," he indignantly accepted. "Apparently when mrmind178 said keeping things off the market is a good way to raise prices, he meant for everyone but him." (LochnessLobster 2005). I pretended to be innocent, but he was right, because that is exactly what I meant. LochnessLobster was furious about my insult of his market principles and my disrespect for his informal authority. For him, it was personal. While the other players continued to discuss their strategies for weeks after his announcement, the RICH guild had broken the strike before they could fully organize, and prices returned to normal. RICH walked away with a healthy profit, and the guild's reputation took a step toward being known as a supplier with low prices.

The first market war was a test of what RICH could do. It only took a few sales to kill the market strike and disrupt the balance in the market. But what if RICH had a never-ending supply? The market strikers believed that they had market power because they had high manufacturing levels and played as honorable players. RICH proved that the market forces did not care about how anyone played the game. The game's official rules and unofficial social conventions provided guidance on what was right and good and honorable, but the market was not concerned about those things. From what I saw, fighting against the market's forces would never be a profitable strategy. My goal was to do what works and avoid what does not work. The market strike did not work.

The Economics (Cartels)

There was one important lesson that I extracted from watching the manufacturers go on strike. These manufacturers, who later called themselves a "Manufacturers' Union," were attempting to manipulate the supply of the game to manipulate the prices in the game. But to do that, they had to understand how supply works, and their assumptions were wrong.

Supply, in economics, is the other side to demand. By definition, an individual supply is the amount of product that an individual or a company is willing to produce at each price, and the market supply is the total of each individual supply all added together. *The law of supply* says that producers will be willing to sell more of their product as the price goes up. The amount of supply also moves as market participants move in and out of the market:

- When more suppliers enter the market, supply goes up, and prices go down.
- When suppliers leave the market, supply goes down, and prices go up.

In the market strike, when the producers left the market to go on strike, the market supply went down. This caused the prices to go up. Over time, the higher prices attracted more producers back into the market. This competition brought more supply into the market and pulled prices back down. What the market strikers were trying to do was form a sort of manufacturing *cartel* (an agreement among suppliers to fix prices) to lock in the amount of supply and fix the manufacturing prices. But these type of agreements only work if everyone involved can be trusted to keep them, and whoever "cheats" the agreement will be the one to walk away with most of the profit. In this case, that was RICH.

Even without RICH, every attempt to form a cartel and increase prices would end with failure. EL had too many suppliers to convince them all to cut back on production. Any empty spots in the market would quickly be filled by whoever chose not to join. One feature of all perfectly competitive markets, like the ones in EL, is that even a large group of suppliers cannot force prices to go higher.

The fundamental instability of cartels, and the fact that they are illegal almost everywhere in the world, makes them uncommon in the real world. The most famous example of a real world cartel is the Organization of the Petroleum Exporting Countries (OPEC). This group of 14 countries contains more than 80 percent of the world's oil reserves and attempts to control the price of oil by coordinating their production and controlling supply. Even this cartel, which has a powerful history, can still be vulnerable to internal disagreement and outside competition from countries that are not part of OPEC (OPEC 2017; OPEC 2018).

CHAPTER 7

The Guild Party

RICH was on its way to becoming the fastest and most efficient production force in the game, but it was also becoming difficult to manage. On June 7, 2005, near the beginning of the manufacturing strike, RICH was officially listed as the largest guild in the game, with 152 members. To direct such a large group of players, I needed to come up with a new way to organize the guild's leadership. But that was easy. The RICH guild's recruiting methods captured some of the smartest players in Eternal Lands (EL), a diverse group of professionals with legitimate real-world experience, most of whom were between 28 and 36 years old:

- seanodonnell and his friend gadai (it means "thief" in Irish), a pair of Irish programmers
- trollson and his colleague Lunksnark, the English rocket engineers (also programmers)
- SiKiK (psychic), an established English banker
- jhunLEMON (John Lennon), a businessman in the Philippines
- JimmyTheSaint, a drug store manager in Alabama
- JoeBlair, a New Yorker who retired young after selling his business
- Protolif, an American soldier and IT expert
- SplargaMan, a mathematician/musician in Colorado
- Eon_Schmidt, a Brazilian programmer

There were more, but you get the idea. It was a group of players who, when they joined RICH, were mostly low-level newbies overlooked by other guilds, but most of them quickly became valuable strategic advisors. Some were also helpful mentors.

Up to this point, RICH had an informal structure. Members flowed between guild projects and naturally separated themselves into different groups. The only thing that I did to facilitate these groups was make sure that RICH had at least one guild leader for every 10 regular members. Because of the types of members that RICH was finding, this ratio was not difficult to maintain, but the next phase of my plan for market control needed more coordination.

The 100,000 fire essences that the guild owned could be sold for a minimum of 350,000 gold coins. That was a lot of gold for such a new guild, but there was more value in using the essences than in selling them, so I held them in my inventory while I thought about what to do next. Fire essences were just the first step in a plan that continued to evolve:

1. Make fire essences.
2. Use fire essences to make metal bars.
3. Use metal bars to make weapons and armor.
4. Sell weapons and armor below market prices.

It was time for step two. It was time to use the fire essences to make metal bars. But how many metal bars? Iron bars required two fire essences, steel bars needed three, and titanium bars used seven. I decided to go for some nice even numbers: 10,000 iron bars, 10,000 steel bars, and 5,000 titanium bars. This would use up 85,000 fire essences, and I could hold the rest for making weapons and armor with manufacturing or gold and silver bars to use in crafting.

This was production on a scale that no other guild had ever imagined before. Even the largest guilds maxed out at about 2,000 total bars at one time, and RICH was aiming for 25,000. There was no comparison, and there was no model for how to achieve that kind of scale. Even harvesting the materials for those metal bars would be more challenging than producing the fire essences: each iron bar took three coal and seven iron ore; every steel bar used five coal and eight iron ore; and every titanium bar required three coal and eight titanium ore. When I added it all up, RICH would have to harvest 95,000 coal, 150,000 iron ore, and 40,000 titanium ore. And this was not like hauling the flowers for the fire essences.

The coal and the ore were *heavy.* The average new player could only haul about 100 coal or 50 iron ore at one time.[1] I needed a new way of organizing the guild's production.

To prepare for this new project, I formalized the guild's leadership group into the "Guild Council" and split RICH into individual units that I labeled as guild houses. These "houses" were separated by skills into manufacturing, crafting, potions, alchemy, and fighting, where each house was responsible for their related skills. With trollson as a main advisor, I took control of the manufacturing and alchemy houses, while SiKiK headed the crafting house and jhunLEMON led the fighting house. Because of the guild's focus on production, the alchemy house was the largest and the fighting house was the smallest. This type of specialization was common in other MMOs, but EL did not have any guilds large enough and focused enough to need it. In EL, RICH would be the first.

The introduction of the guild houses was a minor improvement that led to a radical new form of project organization. I called it the guild party. The guild party was not a political theme. It was simply an event where guild members would gather somewhere, usually a mine, to socialize and make items. This was not a new idea. It was a copy of what I saw when I played with RIVA, and almost every guild used some version of it. The difference was the scale of the RICH parties; while most guilds would have four or five members attending their projects, RICH almost always had 10 or more, and sometimes more than 30.

To start a guild party, the party members would first walk to the edges of the continent and collect the lightest materials for what they were producing. For most essences, it was flowers, but for the steel and iron bars, this meant hours of walking between the coal and iron mines across the Desert Pines. Once the group had enough light materials, they brought everything to the iron mine in the Desert Pines and dropped it in a bag that was close enough to harvest the iron ore. Inside the mine, a high-level guild member would guard the bag from thieves while harvesting the iron ore. The other guild members would take the raw materials out of the bag

---

[1] It was also incredibly slow. Harvesting these materials could take more than twice as long as harvesting flowers and sulfur. It depended on the character's harvesting level.

and mix them into iron bars and steel bars. These parties are how RICH made all 25,000 of the metal bars.

But RICH wasn't only making these metal bars. RICH was making magic essences as well. For the essence parties, I calculated that each member could produce about 10,000 gold coins worth of essences each hour, so I paid a generous 1,000 gold coins per hour.[2] When this was combined with the experience points that the game provided, there was no other guild that could boost a new player this quickly, and the "guildless" players were starting to notice that RICH players were becoming rich players. RICH could recruit for itself without my help.

The Economics (Vertical Integration)

The guild party was a formalized extension of everything that RICH had already been doing:

- It involved each guild member specializing in one specific task.
- The combined effort from all of these players resulted in economies of scale that provided RICH with a production advantage.
- The incentives from earning gold coins and experience points encouraged guild members to participate.

This was all supported by an emphasis on human capital. The next step up, from only producing fire essences to producing metal bars, added a new definition.

By performing multiple steps in the stages of production, and by using slightly different groups of players for each step, the guild was becoming *vertically integrated*. A vertically integrated organization is one

---

[2]My profit calculation was incorrect. I came up with the 10,000 gold coin amount based on what these players could produce, but I did not include the amount of time spent gathering the materials. When my projections were played out in practice, players actually produced about 2,000 to 3,000 gold coins worth of essences per hour. Paying guild members 1,000 gold coins an hour was still profitable, and still more than the zero gold coins that other guilds paid, but it was not as profitable as I had initially assumed.

that does each step of the production process all on its own. It follows the entire production process, from gathering raw materials, to transforming them into intermediate goods, to making and selling the finished goods at the end. This was common in the game world, because almost everyone in EL did every step themselves or as a very small group, but vertically integrated companies can have a huge advantage in the real world.

A classic example of this comes from the Gilded Age, where the Carnegie Steel Company was the king of steel. Already one of the most innovative and efficient steel producers in the world, the company relied on processed coal called "coke coal" to power the furnaces that made its steel. Their coke coal was produced by a company called H. C. Frick & Company. To improve its efficiency even further, the Carnegie Steel Company bought H. C. Frick & Company, creating a vertically integrated company that made Andrew Carnegie the richest man in the world. The reason this move worked so well is because Carnegie Steel had more control over the supply of the inputs for steel production. The company could improve its process of production and transportation, and it could be done cheaper. It also prevented any other steel company from buying out the supplier (Wall 1989).

A more modern version of this idea includes major corporations such as Apple. In the market for computers and phones, there are two layers: the bottom hardware layer, and the software operating layer on top of it. Apple makes hardware (phones, tablets, computers, music players, etc.) and it also makes the core software that goes on top of this hardware. It even sells products in company-branded stores. Apple outsources most of its manufacturing to Foxconn, but it is still considered a vertically integrated company—the hardware layer is branded by Apple, and the operating system layer above it is also branded by Apple. Apple controls both, while most companies do not. Other phone makers rely on Google's Android system, and other computer makers rely on Microsoft's Windows system. In the case of Apple, it has achieved better results by controlling the entire process and the user experience inside the Apple system (Isaacson 2011; Bajarin 2011).

This does not mean that other companies could reach the same level of success using vertical integration, and Apple's vertical integration was actually a danger to the company for part of its history, but it has become one of the company's most successful and enduring features (Knowledge@ Wharton 2012). This factor, combined with a respect for simplistic design, led to Apple becoming the first publicly traded American company to be valued at more than one trillion dollars (Shell 2018).

CHAPTER 8

The Wal-Mart
of Eternal Lands

The guild's membership continued to swell. RICH was everywhere, often gathering in large groups, and its brand was easily recognizable. For low-level players, RICH was highly respected as a very helpful group of people. But to the leadership of other guilds, the ones who felt the pressures of a changing market, RICH was widely considered to be one of the most annoying guilds in the entire game. This attitude might have come from the guild's rocky start, or its recruiting and market strategies (the reasons were always different depending on the time of day), but it became more intense when RICH began unloading finished products.

The 25,000 metal bars that RICH made, if I had decided to sell them, were worth just over one million gold coins. That was more money than I could get from using them to make finished products. But selling these bars would have prevented me from gaining any more experience points from the project, and my primary goal was experience points. The secondary purpose was to prove that my process was better.

The supply of iron, steel, and titanium bars were held in inventory. To start with, I tested the market for almost every item. After experimenting with different items and prices, I came up with some nice round numbers:

- 400 iron helms
- 400 steel shields
- 400 steel chainmail armors
- 400 titanium short swords

These products were all the highest quality manufacturing items that did not use enriched fire essences.[1] I did not know what would sell the fastest. My plan was to make another 100 every time RICH ran out of something, or to stop producing them if they sold too slowly.

The choice to produce those particular items was made easier by the game's fighting system. There was no need for a variety of items because there were no level requirements for who could use which weapons and armor (there were no restrictions on which weapons and armor a player could use), and anyone could buy the best products if they spent enough time harvesting lilacs. This made some of the low-end items almost completely useless, so I already knew that it was not worth trying to sell them. I also knew that if I was able to lower the price far enough, the highest quality weapons and armors would be close enough in price that no one would ever buy the lower quality option.

The way experience points were awarded for fighting also encouraged players to buy the most high-end weapons and armors. When attacking, the same amount of attack experience was given for each hit, no matter how much damage was done.[2] This made swords the wrong choice for earning experience points; the fastest way to level up was by punching the monsters, because using a sword would cause more damage and end the fight without many hits. So, because of the way attack levels were earned, swords were mostly used for attacking other players, not for leveling up, and most people purchased the best sword that they could afford. On the other side, the defense skill actually encouraged using armor. For training, defense experience was given for each dodged attack. Armor allowed players to take less damage when they were hit, which made it possible to stay in the fight longer and potentially dodge more attacks. But there was also a chance that the armor would break and become useless. This forced the fighter to decide which armor would lead to the longest fights.

---

[1] When you know that this game only had about 2,000 or 3,000 players (with about 500 active players online every day), you can see the scale of what RICH was doing. A fair estimate is that RICH could have supplied almost one half of the game's fighters by selling everything from its very first run of production.

[2] The amount of experience depended on the level of the enemy that the player was fighting, but that number was always the same for every hit on the enemy.

The consensus was usually that leather armor offered the best protection for its price.

The result of these features was a market where, as we already know, most of the buyers' decisions were based on price. Most of the game's best items were available to everyone—everyone could afford them and use them—but there was still an established market price, and the suppliers could compete by offering better prices. That was how I planned to compete.

1. Make fire essences.
2. Use fire essences to make metal bars.
3. Use metal bars to make weapons and armor.
4. Sell weapons and armor below market prices.

The first three steps were complete. Everything that RICH was doing happened behind the scenes where nobody could see. Other guilds were aware of the number of players involved, but no one saw where any of the materials were going. Months of discussing, preparing, and producing would finally be converted into gold coins, RICH gold coins, that, according to some rival guilds, completely ruined the game.

The RICH market strategy followed the cycle that I discovered during the guild's creation: charge a price that is slightly lower than the market; buyers are satisfied; lower the price; buyers are satisfied again; lower the price again; but this time it continued until every other producer was pushed out of the market. RICH never ran out of items to sell. The manufacturing market price list looked something like Table 8.1.[3]

RICH was unable to pull down the leather armor prices because NPCs would buy almost every piece of leather armor from producers. If RICH tried to sell below the NPC price, then buyers would just buy from RICH and sell to the NPC for a profit, and there was no reason to

---

[3]Cost calculations for the market could vary by 50 percent or more depending on how players accounted for the cost of food or production failures. Most of the market cost numbers presented in this book were calculated by trollson. The only exception is the high-end items where his model did not accurately match the opportunity cost for production.

Table 8.1 RICH enters the manufacturing market

Manufacturing	Market cost	Market price	RICH price
Armor			
Iron shield	400	400	N/A
Steel shield	462	500	350
Iron helm	214	300	225
Leather helm	25	50	50
Leather pants	58	100	100
Leather boots	83	100	100
Leather torso	181	150	150
Leather gloves	31	45	45
Iron chainmail	557	175	N/A
Steel chainmail	700	1,000	850
Iron cuisses	8,000	8,000	6,000*
Iron greaves	8,000	8,000	6,000*
Iron plate mail	16,000	18,000	13,500*
Weapons			
Iron sword	423	150	N/A
Iron broadsword	546	200	N/A
Steel long sword	649	350	N/A
Steel two-edged sword	837	450	N/A
Titanium short sword	774	625	400
Titanium long sword	8,000	1,000	N/A*
Titanium serpent sword	6,089	10,000	7,000*

*These items used at least one enriched fire essence, which limited the amount of possible mass production, so RICH did not sell them as often.

give away gold coins. For almost everything else, there was no NPC that would buy for any price, and RICH was not artificially limited by how low its prices could go.

RICH did not focus on manufacturing the more expensive weapons and armors that used enriched fire essences. Enriched fire essences were difficult to get in bulk and were often more valuable in other products. For everything else, my pricing scheme was designed to cause the most amount of pain for the other producers while selling my items as fast as possible. But in some cases, the market prices were already forcing

THE WAL-MART OF ETERNAL LANDS   59

producers to sell at a loss. There were two features of the game that caused this phenomenon:

1. Producers were rewarded with experience points for everything they produced, but they would only get gold coins if they chose to sell their products. Sometimes a player decided that the experience alone was good enough for them, and they would be willing to sell for a lower price. RICH was part of this category.
2. Fighters could also get swords that were dropped by monsters. They would also be willing to sell these for less because they didn't use any extra effort to get the swords. This is why the titanium long sword sold for such a low price compared to its cost.

It was a market where prices were somewhat fixed, but players could still compete within the price limits set by NPCs. And because quality wasn't a factor (aside from the difference between different types of swords and armors), the customers would always take the cheapest offer. RICH was now, *by far*, the cheapest offer. RICH was no longer the annoying startup that poked LochnessLobster's manufacturing strike. RICH had become something much more dangerous. RICH, as a guild, earned its unofficial label as the Wal-Mart of Eternal Lands. It was transitioning into a large force in the market.

The Economics (Normal Goods and Inferior Goods)

This is the first chapter that fully explores the mysteries of the EL manufacturing market. The prices in the market are set by the intersection of supply and demand, but supply and demand for each individual item is influenced by other factors outside its own market. We've already described how these markets can resemble perfectly competitive markets, so we know that the only successful way to compete was by price.

For weapons and armor, there is a clear difference in which items are better than others. The easiest way to see the difference is in the markets for iron shields and steel shields. We don't need to worry about how much better a steel shield is; it's enough to know that it is better, and we can see this because people are still willing to buy it at a higher price. For the

Table 8.2 The RICH Effect on the shield market

Manufacturing	Market cost	Market price	RICH price
Armor			
Iron shield	400	400	N/A
Steel shield	462	500	350

market (before RICH), an iron shield was priced at 400 gold coins and a steel shield was priced at 500 gold coins (as shown in Table 8.2).

In general, when there are two items of different quality, the lower quality items are considered *inferior goods*. This means that people will buy less of them as their income goes up, because they are trading up to the next level of quality. For EL, a player with more income would trade up from iron shields to steel shields. The iron shields were an inferior good, and steel shields were a *normal good*. A normal good is one that people will buy more of as their income goes up. A simple example in the real world is basic foods such as spam. As a person's income goes up, they'll switch away from the low-quality spam and start buying better meat. That is what we mean when we compare inferior goods to normal goods. Spam is an inferior good, not because it is lower quality, but simply because people will buy less when their income goes up.

It's not only income that will encourage someone to step up to a higher quality item. If the price of one similar item changes, it will shift the demand for the other item. RICH was able to lower the price of a steel shield from 500 to 350. RICH did not sell iron shields, and the market abandoned iron shields. There were two economic reasons behind this:

1. Iron shields and steel shields are considered *substitute goods*, because one can be switched out and replaced with the other.[4] This creates what is called a *substitution effect*. Lowering the price of the steel shields reduces the demand for the iron shields.

[4]Some of the items in EL could be considered *complement goods*, which means that they are generally bought at the same time and are used together, but it is not as clear. For example, players would often buy multiple pieces of different leather armor (pants, torso, gloves, helmet) all at the same time.

2. Lowering the price of the steel shields also generated an *income effect*, because lowering the price is basically the same as increasing income. Lower prices or higher income both make it possible to buy more. A player could buy two steel shields from RICH for 700 total gold coins, or they could buy one steel shield for 500 gold coins in the market (or two iron shields for 800, if they really wanted to). The RICH deal was better.

But there was a limit to what RICH could do, and that limit was set by the NPCs. An NPC set the price for almost every piece of leather armor, and RICH made little effort to alter the leather armor market prices, as shown in Table 8.3.

Table 8.3 The RICH Effect on the market for leather armor

Manufacturing	Market cost	Market price	RICH price*
Armor			
Leather helm	25	50	50
Leather pants	58	100	100
Leather boots	83	100	100
Leather torso	181	150	150
Leather gloves	31	45	45

* Sometimes RICH sold leather armors a bit lower than the market prices, but not consistently. They were the most popular way to level up and the most popular armor to buy, so the market was much larger than the other armors.

The NPCs were setting a price floor on most pieces of leather armor in the same way that they set a price floor on lilacs: by purchasing them from players. Almost everyone would sell to the NPC if the market price was too close to the NPC price. If the market somehow tried to go below the NPC price, then players would buy from the market and sell to the NPCs. This is called *arbitrage*, and it is one way that markets become more efficient. Buying from the market and selling to NPCs would pull the market prices to the same level as the NPC prices.

In the bigger picture, market prices were usually lower than market costs. This is because there was a hidden benefit that was rarely included in cost calculations. What most people were missing was the one thing that RICH exploited more than anything else. Experience points have value, and including the value of experience points makes it perfectly rational for players to be willing to sell their products for less than the market price. And, as we already know, low-level players valued experience more than high-level players, so they should be willing to sell for even lower prices. RICH was primarily low-level players who wanted to level up.

This gave RICH an extra boost from its focus on low-level players. Having low-level players now meant that RICH would have two major advantages: a production advantage from its vertical integration and economies of scale; and an extra pricing advantage from the value of experience. But there is one other more subtle difference that was beginning to show. As RICH continued to recruit the inexperienced players that no one else wanted to take, the investments in human capital meant that RICH members were becoming as powerful as the elite players that other guilds normally recruited. In the market for guild members, RICH had sold itself to low-level players who became high-level players. When they became high-level players, they didn't leave RICH, and they certainly did not join another guild. It was a hidden way of reducing the number of potential guild members for every other guild. RICH was taking all of the new players and preventing other guilds from growing, but the other guilds could not see this because they did not realize that every elite player started as a new player.

None of this explains why RICH would choose to sell for prices that are 30 percent to 50 percent lower than the normal market prices. RICH could have been more like RIVA and sold at the established market prices. RICH could have still made money by selling closer to the normal market prices. Any higher prices could have potentially been more profitable than what RICH chose, even as a high-volume, low-margin producer. It was also a somewhat risky strategy, because RICH could have run out of items to sell, and the effort would have been wasted. It was unnecessary and probably less profitable than what was optimal. The reason behind such dramatically low prices was not strategic. It was hostile. RICH was engaging in what is called *predatory pricing*. This is when a producer decides to sell for lower prices with the intention of driving competitors out of business.

In the real world, the company most often accused of predatory pricing is Wal-Mart. On the surface, that would make RICH the Wal-Mart of Eternal Lands. It's a good comparison, but also incomplete. RICH was a manufacturer, not just a seller. In the modern world, Wal-Mart is the closest to RICH and a major theme for how RICH was viewed inside the game. If we go back about 100 years, we can find others that match more closely, such as John Rockefeller's Standard Oil[5] or Andrew Carnegie's Carnegie Steel Company, but Wal-Mart was close enough to be the label that stuck (Chernow 1998; Economist 1999; Fishman 2007).

[5]Standard Oil was well-known as a company that would threaten to cut prices to take out competitors. The competition was always given the option of getting crushed or getting bought out, and competitors almost always recognized that they would not win a market war against John Rockefeller.

CHAPTER 9

The Crafting Market Collapse

The manufacturing market was getting wiped out, but I was motivated to go farther. It was not enough just to be rich. I still needed to prove that my process was sustainable, and I needed to show that I could duplicate my methods in other markets. My next target was the alchemy market. Alchemy was a step in the process to manufacturing, which made it easy to adapt the guild party method for other alchemy products. For this market, I chose to have the guild focus on offering contracts for large batches of the most popular alchemy products. But RICH would only sell the end products, such as health essences (used in magic for healing), not middle-step products, such as metal bars, because the metal bars had more value at the next step of production. I also made sure that the guild kept any of the valuable enriched essences that came out of these projects.

After testing my idea with several private contracts, I established the guild's market presence in an advertisement published on July 21, 2005 in the marketplace section of the official EL forums.

> After a few private dealings, RICH is now going public. We will make by special order any manufacturable item, any essence, or any ring/medallion. The catch to this is that *we don't do small orders.*
>
> If you are interested in a bulk order for alchemy/manu/crafting services, PM me or another RICH member (preferably gadai, sikik, seanodonnell, jimmythesaint, salun, or jhunlemon) in game and we will work out some sort of deal. Tell us the item you need, the amount you want, and the price you're looking for. If it is not acceptable for us, we will not do it. (Mr.Mind 2005)

I said that we would make anything but bars or potions, but essences were the only products that EL players ever ordered in large quantities.

I also came up with a new way of competing. Alchemy was a massive market, and it had a unique source of extra demand. EL had a game store on its website where players could buy gold and rare items for real-world money (selling in-game items for real money was not possible, but players could buy them from Entropy). Most of the RICH alchemy customers bought their gold from this store, and they were willing to pay a higher price to get their essences faster. This made it possible for RICH to charge premium prices for faster delivery (Table 9.1 shows the prices that RICH used for alchemy products).

Table 9.1 RICH enters the alchemy market

Alchemy	Market cost	Market price	RICH price[*]
Essences			
Fire essence	1.6	3.5	N/A
Magic essence	4.7	8.0	8.0
Air essence	6.0	7.0	N/A
Health essence	3.9	7.0	7.0
Life essence	3.1	5.0	6.0
Energy essence	5.1	6.0	6.0
Spirit essence	18.1	9.0	N/A
Matter essence	6.3	7.0	7.0
Water essence	5.1	6.0	6.0
Death essence	15.6	15.0	15.0
Earth essence	4.1	3.8	N/A
Metal Bars			
Iron bar	28	38	N/A
Steel bar	35	43	N/A
Titanium bar	60	45	N/A
Silver bar	24	38	N/A
Gold bar	40	42	N/A

[*]Prices varied based on the size and timing of the order, but RICH rarely sold alchemy products below the market rate. Price competition was not necessary, because it was an on-demand service in very high volume with customers that cared more about speed than price. Almost all alchemy orders were for health essences (used for healing) and life essences (used for summoning).
RICH did not sell metal bars because they were more valuable to the guild when converted into weapons, armor, and jewelry. Fire essences were also more valuable at the next step.

RICH was fast. The guild could begin a project at night with Americans, pass it on to the Australian side, and have it finished by the Europeans by the next morning. It was a remarkable amount of dedication that no other guild could duplicate. And even if they wanted to, none of them had enough guild members spread throughout the world.[1] It made the guild so fast that some of the RICH customers didn't even have their money before their orders were filled. RICH could make tens of thousands of essences faster than Entropy could fill a real money purchase order.

The trick that I used went beyond RICH. Since I still paid the RICH members who attended the parties, I decided to invite other guilds to help RICH make essences. This way, I could have more workers who I didn't have to pay; they came for the party and the experience points, and RICH walked away with the products and the gold coins. But it was even more than that. I also invited *unfriendly* guilds to the RICH parties. Some of the RICH guild's most outspoken critics, even the ones who cynically compared RICH to Wal-Mart, found themselves in a mine, surrounded by RICH members, producing RICH products.

The power of experience points was the power of RICH. It attracted a dozen new players to the guild every week, and it charmed the RICH enemies into helping a guild that they hated. The temptation of experience points was so powerful that even the people who hated RICH were compelled to join the party. And they didn't care if they got paid, because the experience points were sufficient. This allowed the guild to add extra workers without any extra cost. And, after watching this happen for several RICH parties, I completely quit offering gold coin payments. The experience points alone proved to be enough of an incentive for both RICH members and for their party guests. For guild members, the gold coin payments were replaced by free manufactured items. The guild became, for its members, a massive storage full of items, and anything that they needed, no matter what it was, was available *for free*.

Around the same time that the guild entered the alchemy market, I began to review the crafting market. Crafting was a lot like

---

[1] It's unlikely that anyone even knew what RICH was doing. The RICH way of managing these large projects was not generally shared with anyone outside the guild.

manufacturing. The buyers were fighters looking to supplement their armor and weapons with enchanted jewelry. The suppliers, a relatively small group, were often crafting specialists with no other skills. The similarities, however, distracted me from one critical difference between the crafting market and the manufacturing market. Crafting items, in most cases, were an unnecessary novelty, and the market was much smaller. I would learn this the hard way.

Although the market was small, the people who specialized in crafting could still make some money, and I thought it would be easy for RICH to capture some of these profits. To prepare, the RICH alchemy house had already produced about 2,000 silver bars and 2,000 gold bars. The rest was up to the guild's crafting house. They worked together to provide a continuous supply of crafting materials. My only decision was what to sell and when to sell it.

I tried to repeat my manufacturing strategy. I made 400 of every crafting item and tried to cut the price by a little at a time. But it didn't work in the same way. This time, RICH was bigger than the market. Instead of a stable steady decline in prices, the crafting market collapsed. Some of the medallions were so oversupplied that their market price dropped *all the way to zero!* What RICH had introduced to the crafting market completely overwhelmed everything that the consumers were willing to buy!

The result was more incredible than I imagined. What RICH had done to the crafting market, by pulling some prices all the way to zero, was both a mistake and an announcement that RICH was a serious threat to the integrity of the game. It was a mistake because I chose the wrong items to sell, but that was easy to correct. The moon medallion was so much better than the others (it had the same benefits as two medallions combined) that it was usually the only one that players wanted to buy. The only reason that the other medallions had any market value was because crafting specialists were slowly selling off their supply. Now, because of RICH, they could not even give them away. Neither could I. After a few days at zero prices, the market for the other medallions eventually cleared out, and RICH was able to establish reasonable prices. The end result was an elegant pricing scheme, as shown in Table 9.2.

The market was crushed so thoroughly that, instead of trying to fight, the crafting specialists walked away from it, and RICH was the only one still

Table 9.2 RICH enters the crafting market

Crafting	Market cost	Market price	RICH price*
Gems			
Polished sapphire	31	18	N/A
Polished ruby	31	18	N/A
Polished emerald	30	14	N/A
Polished diamond	59	35	N/A
Rings			
Gold ring	113	75	N/A
Silver ring	71	75	N/A
Disengagement ring	143	110	70
Desert Pines teleport	197	90	65
VOTD teleport	177	100	65
Isla Prima teleport	139	90	65
Naralik teleport	179	90	65
Whitestone teleport	196	90	65
Portland teleport	197	90	65
Damage ring	143	110	70
Medallions			
Silver medallion	103	125	N/A
Gold medallion	167	125	N/A
Unicorn medallion	176	250	150
Sun medallion	284	250	150
Moon medallion	186	300	150
Stars medallion	186	300	150

*Gems, basic rings, and basic medallions were not the end point of the crafting process, so RICH did not sell them.

standing. Even RICH was forced to stop producing any medallions other than moon medallions. But it still made money on the rest. In fact, RICH made money on almost everything, but it still could not sell while I was asleep.

The Economics (Supply and Demand Shifters)

The RICH entry to the crafting market was an experiment, but it was also guided by economics. Looking back through the lens of economic theory, there are a few reasons why the crafting market imploded. At first, the numbers that stand out the most are the ones that were not affected by RICH. RICH never sold gems or metal bars because they were intermediate goods used to make other products, and there was more value in taking the next step. This made RICH vertically integrated for crafting in the same way that it was vertically integrated for manufacturing. RICH controlled the entire manufacturing and crafting process all the way from harvesting the basic materials to selling the end products.

RICH sold essences but did not compete by price. Essences were *consumable goods*, one-use items that disappeared after they were used, and their demand was more stable (teleport rings were also consumables, but it was a small market). The other products—weapons, armor, and medallions—were all *durable goods* that lasted for a long time. RICH could produce durable goods faster than the game used them up.

The other part of this informal experiment was a unique interaction between supply and demand. Demand is influenced by outside factors (called *demand shifters*) such as:

- the price and quality of related products;
- buyers entering or leaving the market; and
- changes in income.

The moon medallion was a substitute for the other medallions that would cause a shift in demand for the other medallions. Dropping its price would lower the demand (and therefore the price) for the other medallions. Part of the reason why it was so destructive is a concept called *elasticity*. Elasticity measures how much the sales of a product respond to a change in price. The more responsive the product is to a change in price, the more elastic it is. For the crafting market, the biggest effect came from a specific type of elasticity called the *cross-price elasticity of demand*. This measures how much the demand for a product changes when the price of another product changes. The medallions were very responsive to a change in price of the moon medallion, and it caused the market to collapse.

On the other side, supply can be influenced by *supply shifters* such as:

- the number of producers entering or leaving the market;
- new technology or production methods;

- the prices of what is used to make products; and
- producers' future expectations for the market.

RICH represented a new source of supply with a better production method (the guild party). It was effectively increasing the supply for every ring, medallion, weapon, and armor that it sold (and therefore lowering the price).

In the end, this was an even more extreme case of predatory pricing than the manufacturing market. RICH ruined everyone else in the market, and transformed the crafting market into a *monopoly*. Most people are familiar with the idea of a monopoly; it's when one firm is the only supplier in the market. In the crafting market, RICH was a special type of monopoly called a *natural monopoly*. A natural monopoly is a market where one company can produce its products at a lower cost than any other potential competitor. In the real world, the type of business that tends to favor a natural monopoly is one with a high barrier to entry caused by high startup costs. This includes industries like electricity, telephone, Internet, or railroads. In EL, the barriers to entry were relatively low, so anyone could sell their products to the market. But there was a barrier to making money. RICH had such significantly lower costs that anyone attempting to compete with RICH would be guaranteed to lose money unless they changed their methods and added more guild members.

These other guilds could never compete, because even if they improved their process, RICH had already lured their members into working at the essences parties. In economic terms, the RICH move into the alchemy and crafting markets was a form of *horizontal integration*, and the ability to recruit other guilds' members contributed to the effect (by further lowering the RICH labor costs). Horizontal integration is just an attempt to concentrate power at the same stage of production. In the real world, Disney provides an excellent example of horizontal integration; the company has made several major acquisitions over the past few years, including Pixar, Marvel, Lucasfilm, and 20th Century Fox (Crunchbase Inc. 2018). These are all businesses operating in the same market as Disney's movie and TV production studios. With its moves into crafting and alchemy, RICH had Wal-Mart's prices and Disney's magic.

CHAPTER 10

The RICH Effect

Despite RICH controlling every EL market, and listing over 150 members, RICH was unable to cover the whole world. There were rumors about a cycle that players began calling "The RICH Effect." When I was online, the game would have RICH prices, and normal market prices returned when I stopped selling every night. Desperate manufacturers pushed themselves to only do business with the other side of the world. While I slept, market prices supposedly jumped up to "normal," and they retreated back down to the "RICH level" when I came back online. The guild needed some way to ensure that every player had access to RICH prices. The best way that I could think of was by using a trading bot.

Bots were similar to the NPCs. The major difference is that they were characters created by players instead of by Entropy. They were run by a program that the owner uses to set their functions, and the two most popular types of bots were administrative bots and trade bots. The administrative bots helped coordinate guild activities and trade bots allowed guilds to sell items automatically.

There were some challenges to owning a trading bot:

- The bot's owner needed to know how to write computer code.
- The owner had to pay Entropy a $20 fee (or $100 for a bot with a larger store).
- The bot could not move from its designated spot.

However, because of a loophole in the rules, all three of these conditions could be overlooked by having the bot be designated as an "alternate character." An alternate character was legal as long as the owner never directly traded with that character. If they directly traded with an alternate character, then they would be breaking one of EL's official rules.

Richery, whose name is a combination of the words "rich" and "treasury" (not "rich" and "trickery," like most people believed) became the guild's trade bot by default. He was created to be the guild storage, where the RICH guild could hold everything that it owned all in one place. The game did not have an easy way for players to share items.

Despite having several programmers in the guild, it would take RICH months to code a bot program for Richery, and I didn't have the $100 needed to make him an official bot. Because having a coded bot seemed to be too far in the future, I decided to control Richery myself. I would use him as both an unofficial trade bot and as a guild storage. I would allow the daily RICH Effect cycle to continue until Richery could become an official trade bot.

Richery, while not an official trading bot, still functioned mostly within the rules as an alternate character. The game rules said that I could not trade with him directly while I controlled him, but I could have someone else sign in as Richery and trade with that person, or I could have Richery trade with a middleman who traded with me. The rules were meant to prevent players from having multiple characters working together, but they limited how much a guild like RICH could work together as a group of people. RICH considered Richery a guild-owned character, and his purpose was to make it easier to manage the guild.

I was often too impatient to take all of the steps necessary to keep Richery legal as an alternate character. Occasionally, just to speed things up a bit, I would trade with him directly. I was not getting caught, so I kept doing it more often and more brazenly. I even started bragging about how I was getting away with it. I started thinking that I might be too powerful to be punished. I wasn't.

The one day—*the one time*—that an EL moderator purchased something from Richery's store, I pushed my luck a little too far. When the moderator questioned Richery's purpose and function, I described how he was a guild-owned character similar to other guilds' trading characters, and I asked the moderator if using Richery as the guild's selling character was acceptable. Their response confirmed it. "Well yes. But you MUST not trade with yourself between the two characters. That is highly illegal."

"I don't." I lied.[1] Everyone knew that I was trading with Richery when it was more convenient. Even the moderators knew it. But they could not prove it, and I had escaped from any serious punishment every time they questioned me. I was so open about what I was doing that it was almost an offense to their moderator powers. I also didn't think I was wrong. I justified it by making it known that his purpose was to hold things for the guild, and he was not helping the guild manufacture items or harvest resources. Technically, the game allowed sharing items between characters, but not always the way I was doing it.

The moderator was sitting next to me in a place called the Tarensgaard storage building, inside a distant city just past the Valley of the Dwarves (VOTD), and he was looking to buy some steel shields. After Richery arrived and finished the sale, I noticed that his stock of steel shields was almost empty and needed to be restored. Using the alternate character loophole would have taken a few minutes longer than I wanted to wait, so I chose to speed things up. I directly traded with Richery, giving him another 100 new steel shields to sell.

This trade was openly breaking the rules, but I was confident that no one would see it. It was also an extra risky move, because I was standing between two moderators when I made the trade. I was aware of the punishment for "illegal multiplay," and I had just confirmed that it was highly illegal, but I was pretty sure that they were not looking. Even if they saw me, I didn't think there was anything they could do, because they had never been able to do anything before. But I was wrong. This time they were watching me. They were expecting me to break this rule. And no, I was not above the law.

Richery began walking to the Desert Pines, but he only made it to the docks in the VOTD before he froze, was disconnected, and booted from the game. Richery was banned! Everything that Richery was holding, the millions the guild owned, was gone.

The two moderators who made the decision, still sitting next to me in the Tarensgaard storage, stood up to tell me why. Another one walked in to join them. The three of them used it as an opportunity to give me

---

[1] The public record of this conversation exists in the Eternal Lands Official Forums as a comment about Richery (Mr.Mind 2005).

a 1-hour lecture on fair play. They had accepted the original structure behind Richery's operation, but this did not fall within those rules. What I just did, according to the moderators, was the most serious crime that can be committed in EL.

gadai, the Irish programmer who had followed seanodonnell into the guild, was enraged. Richery was also holding 80,000 gold coins worth of gadai's gear and materials. gadai did nothing wrong, and he stepped in to plead on behalf of the guild.

But it didn't matter what anyone said. The moderators would not change their minds. No exception would be made, not even to rescue the items that Richery was holding for other people, not even to save gadai's gear. The entire RICH operation that flowed through Richery was completely frozen.

I was stunned by their decisiveness. The moderators, a group that never liked my public contempt for their authority, finally found a way to shut me down. Richery held everything that RICH owned. When Richery went down, the materials he had been storing for the guild went with him. What made it even worse was that there was no way to get anything back, because appealing their decision was also against the rules!

It might have been against the rules to appeal, but the benefits from trying were worth more than losing everything forever. From reading the forums, I knew that Entropy's enforcement of the rules was much more forgiving, and he seemed to like RICH. I thought he would accept an appeal if there was an opportunity for compromise.

On July 24, 2005, I made a post in the official EL forums asking for forgiveness. After an explanation of Richery's function and purpose, I left it up to the moderators. "I ask only one thing. That Richery be unlocked so that he can continue trading *as a legal character*. There were no intentions of illegal multiplaying, and I was not benefitting from this as people do from muling." (Mr.Mind 2005)[2]

My post only attracted more scrutiny from the moderators.

---

[2]Muling in EL meant using an alternate character to harvest and carry resources from a mine to a storage. Richery was not used that way.

Not only did you lie, you understood that you were doing something illegal. ... You have had too many chances, and you should count yourself lucky that your main character was not banned. (Placid 2005)

I can't imagine how you can claim ignorance of the rules. (Aislinn 2005)

I'm sorry Mr.Mind, were you somehow unable to read the rules of this game? ... Your own conversations have been proof enough that you know of the illegality of your actions. Buy a store bot. Play by the rules. (Ghrae 2005)

trollson offered an appeal.

This doesn't just affect Mr.Mind; Richery stored the goods for the entire Guild—some 150 innocent players/characters have been affected by the ban. ... Whatever happens to Richery the character, we would really appreciate that the Guild assets are returned somehow. ... Richery was serving a purpose due to a shortcoming in the game—namely no Guild storage facility. Such a facility is sorely needed for those guilds intent on mercantile activities. (trollson 2005)

The moderators were not swayed by his arguments.

If you have issues, you really all need to take them up with your guild leader. It is unfortunate that you have all lost items, but it is more unfortunate that your guild leader chose to gamble with your belongings in this way. (Aislinn 2005)

trollson clarified the guild's position. "So the perception we* have is that due to a technical infringement** the assets of *c.*150 hard-working honest players/characters have been effectively seized." (trollson 2005).

The moderators countered.

Let's get it right: *Many* *technical infringements* over a *long* period of time, which the *guild leader no less,* has done. ... [You should talk] with your guild leader about why you all are in his guild in the first place if he is playing so carelessly with your trust and belongings. (Aislinn 2005)[3]

The moderators may not have been convinced, but their opinions did not matter. It was Entropy who made the final decision, and he agreed on a compromise. "If you pay 20 USD (to have the right to use it as a commerce bot), or if you pay 100 USD (have the right to use it as a commerce bot with huge carry load) then I will unban it." (Entropy 2005).

Paying a fee to take Richery's status from unofficial to official, when the alternative was having him banned, was a fair deal. I did not have the money (which was the main reason why I never registered him before), but SiKiK, the guild's banker, offered to pay $100 to register Richery as a bot. RICH effectively got off with a fine. It was the kind of resolution that I had been betting on.

After becoming a registered trade bot, Richery was appropriately placed in the abandoned Portland Bank. The location was fitting but also somewhat restricting. The game's main market area was in the VOTD, not Portland, and there were trading bots on almost every random corner, so a somewhat obscure location would mean that other bots would be seen first. But using the Portland Bank gave Richery his own store space with an atmosphere that was fitting for a RICH guild. It had shelves covered in rare gems and bags of money, and a desk with a bag of money, an appropriate setting for a bot named Richery that carried the RICH guild tag. Of course, now that he could no longer move, the buyers would have to find him. But as long as his prices were unbeatable, all he needed to do was tell the customers how to get to the Portland Bank.

For a small fee of one enriched fire essence per month, a friendly guild agreed to run Richery's trading services through their server using their code, allowing him to automatically announce his prices in the game's market channel and trade with the players who came to his Portland Bank. This made it possible for him to be active in the market at any hour of the day by announcing RICH prices in the market channel and selling

---

[3]There were high-level guild leaders who reminded me of my responsibility, but no one ever questioned their commitment to RICH.

RICH goods. With a newly automated Richery representing the guild, The RICH Effect became permanent.

The Economics (Regulatory Barrier to Entry)

The RICH Effect, in the context of economic theory, was really just a supply shift that happened every day. One of the causes for a supply shift is when a competitor enters or leaves a market. When I came online, RICH was in the market. This caused the supply to increase and the prices to go down. When I went offline, RICH was out of the market. This caused supply to decrease and prices to go up. Because this pattern was predictable, it would have been possible for players to arbitrage the difference between the day's prices and the night's prices, but no one ever did. Instead, they usually just waited for the best time to sell their own products. When Richery came online, the game's prices became more stable throughout the day, and the markets became more efficient overall. It was an improvement.

There is one item that we have enough data on to track the power of The RICH Effect in the manufacturing market. The iron helm fell from a market price of 300 gold coins before RICH entered the market down to 225 after RICH entered the market, and finally down to 175 after Richery was proven to be a stable supplier.[4] The market cost for an iron helm stayed around 214 gold coins throughout this entire period, so this was one of the few items that RICH did not initially sell "at a loss," but it eventually fell victim to The RICH Effect. At 175, a supplier would lose 39 gold coins for each iron helm. When the price was 300, they were making 86 gold coins on each sale. It was a dramatic difference by the numbers, and it made everyone severely uncomfortable when they saw their profits disappear.

Richery would inevitably become controversial, but the bigger question for this part of the story is why I would assume that RICH was too powerful to be punished. It was a dangerous assumption to test, because it implied that the enforcement of EL rules could be corrupted. It was

---

[4]It dropped all the way down to 150 after RICH found a better production method, but that came later in the story.

also an inappropriate gamble, because if I was wrong, then RICH could lose everything. Even if I was right, the most that RICH could potentially gain would be a spark to change the rule to make room for a guild storage character (I should have done a cost-benefit analysis). Ultimately, I was both wrong and right. The moderators were enforcing the rules by the book, but Entropy encouraged more creative ways of playing his game, and Richery was justifiably overcoming a limitation in the game that Entropy started working to solve. Whether the $100 payment was a fine or a bribe depends on who you ask, but Entropy made the rules, and he felt that it was fair. [5]

The issue is a little more nuanced than just a disregard for the rules. The payment for registering a bot was what economists consider a *regulatory barrier to entry*. Unlike high startup costs, this is a barrier to entry that is created and supported by government regulations. They are not all distinctly good or bad, and they do not stay good or bad forever. In EL, it was a barrier that I did not have the resources to overcome, but it was entirely reasonable for Entropy to expect some payment in exchange for the bots that were populating his game; he would be compensated for the space they used, and the game could be artificially prevented from overcrowding. In the real world, there are hundreds of examples, including any business that requires a license, such as doctors. There are also larger businesses, such as utilities, with government-protected competitive positions. Sometimes these limitations ensure the quality of the product or service that is provided, but sometimes they simply allow a uniquely inefficient business to continue operating inefficiently. It depends on the market.

---

[5]Events like this are interesting because the public record only exists as a result of my misjudgment. It was bad at the time but good for recording history.

CHAPTER 11

Market War II

The ruthless efficiency that generated The RICH Effect was enhanced by the trading system created by bots. Before Richery entered the market, prices would fluctuate depending on which producers were available, but a bot could sell items at any time, day or night. And after the spread of bots such as Richery, the market prices became more stable throughout the day. In other words, the whole market became more efficient.

The market's increasing concentration and efficiency led to a simple structural change. It started with lots of competitors, but the rise of RICH transformed the market into a monopoly. Whenever RICH lowered its prices, everyone else would be forced to follow. If they could not match the RICH prices, then they would be forced to leave the market. There are no numbers for the whole game, but everyone recognized RICH as the dominant producer. RICH was at the top of Eternal Lands (EL).

The shift in the crafting market was more painful than the others. It was barely big enough to handle the supply even before RICH entered the market, and the strain of adding Richery to the market made almost everyone else invisible. It was a situation that EL's leading crafting specialists could not accept. On September 28, 2005, the anger boiled over into a crafting strike, this time led by EL's highest level crafter, DrMabuse. The idea was identical to what LochnessLobster proposed for manufacturing—no one involved with crafting could supply their services until the market cleared out and favorable prices came back. This time, I didn't leave any doubts about my position.

"The prices for teleport, damage, and disengagement rings + medallions are in my eyes too low." announced DrMabuse. He provided examples, citing RICH prices and calling them insane. Then he continued, "I am (crafting level 45) on strike. I am not crazy and do all the work (harvest ore, make bars + fire essences, make rings) for such low prices." (DrMabuse 2005).

I quickly confirmed, "I am not joining the strike," and let the conversation go on without me (Mr.Mind 2005).

As the conversation heated up, including one player who said they "almost cried" because the prices were so low, more rational voices trickled in. The biggest in the crafting market was Ghrae, a highly respected moderator whose words would carry some weight. He agreed that there was a problem. "I'm a top level crafter. And yes, the market for items is horrible. ... And lately, I can't make a profit. It sucks, I admit." But he disagreed with what DrMabuse proposed.

> However, I don't believe in a strike either. It's a pretty face for price manipulation. It's a form of trying to control the market. But what does it really do? It allows those who do NOT participate in the strike to find easy buyers. (Ghrae 2005)

His view was that a strike would only help the people who stayed in the market, a point that was proven during the manufacturing strike.

LochnessLobster offered his emotional support. "Although my crafting is -0- I have often thought that crafting would be the only skill worse than manufacturing as far as the market goes. You have my support for what it's worth." (LochnessLobster 2005).

LadyWolf, one of the RICH guild's harshest critics, offered her own perspective.

> I have all but stopped crafting (level 31). ... It's gotten to where I barely break even. ... When I started playing 8 months ago (approximately), [disengagement] rings sold for 100–120 each, now, we are lucky to get 75–80 for them. (LadyWolf 2005)

She joined the strike.

After a few other players offered their perspectives, both in support and with critical questions, DrMabuse came back to thank them for their attention. "**Attention** is one goal of the strike. Second goal is to inform about a **serious economic unfairness**." He went on to demonstrate the costs of making teleport rings. By his calculations, a VOTD ring could cost 142 gold coins to make, but RICH was selling them for 65. That was unfair to everyone else (DrMabuse 2005).

LadyWolf added her own conclusion.

> Well, MrMind said he wants to be like Walmart. Walmart is what has put the little guy out of business [in real life]. Except in game, we can't draw unemployment when our jobs get taken away from us. ... [Bots like Richery] seem to be trying to undercut all the others to soak up all the gold for their guilds, thus hurting those of us that don't rely on a bot to sell for us. (LadyWolf 2005)

She refused to do business with RICH, and came back later to add, "MrMind doesn't care, he's out to destroy the market. It's a petty game he's playing, and only a set price cap will stop him." (LadyWolf 2005).

gadai countered the attack on Richery's business.

> Richery was set to buy at a certain price point, well below market rate. In all, less than 100 [disengagement] rings and 500 location rings were sold to Richery by RICH guild members, yet in his brief time trading (less than three weeks) he had a turnover of more than 3.5k rings. Before blaming the RICH guild or even MrMind I suggest having a pop at whatever mass crafters sold to him. Considering 2,000 of those rings were [disengagement] rings I would suspect that at least one of the sellers is in the top 50 crafters. (gadai 2005)

The topic continued to draw interest for a few days, but it became calmer when Entropy promised that a solution called cooldown was being considered, and hinted that major changes were coming. The arguments against a strike were definitively shut down by a neutral player called TheDoctor, who said,

> This strike is going to fail: MrMind sells [disengagement]/damage rings at 70 [gold coins], teleport rings at 65, and medallions at 150. Those are the cheapest prices in the game. He is well advertised, and everyone will just go to him. (TheDoctor 2005)

In the end, TheDoctor was right. Nobody who was unable to lower their costs would ever be able compete with Richery. But the crafting strike supporters were not satisfied with that conclusion. They followed me into another topic where RICH was advertising its prices. There, they continued to protest the RICH impact on the market.

> RICH is one of the reasons for the crafters' strike. We already make less than the cost price … and RICH is undercutting by a lot. In part, this was done by their bot (as in selling, not as in cheating) as such, I'm asking people to boycott RICH. (ttlanhil 2005)

gadai mounted a reasonable defense.

The prices slipped down long before Richery ever came to the market, but that bot seems to provide everyone with a convenient scapegoat for craft/manu prices. Thank goodness the bot never sold essences or we'd be blamed for that too! The higher the levels of crafters/manufacturers and the more people that start practicing those skills … the more of these goods enter the market and the lower the price. (gadai 2005)

The market strikers had a response ready. "I know other bots undercut prices as well, but (1) not by as much (as far as I've seen) and (2) they (bots/owners/guilds) are so far in support of the strike for better prices or haven't commented." (ttlanhil 2005).

gadai had an answer.

Do you honestly expect anyone to post against this strike— excepting of course MrMind (who is doing it for his own mysterious reasons) and I (who am too foolish to keep my trap shut). The majority of bot owners, even if they were against your proposals, wouldn't post to say so for fear of drawing ill will upon themselves— why do it? (gadai 2005)

gadai was unaware that my "mysterious reason" was actually because I enjoyed drawing ill will upon myself (and also, more attention meant more business, especially if it was directed at my low prices), but he presented me with an opportunity to jump into the conversation.

I needed to be clear that these players could not affect RICH in the same way that Ember's boycott had devastated the guild. "This boycott will never succeed because the customer base we have either does not read the forums, does not care what other people are paying, wants the best price, or has nothing against me." (Mr.Mind 2005).

The crafters were skeptical. "Rich sells ring of portland for 65 [gold coins], right?" They added up the costs and determined that the cheapest it could possibly be made was for 68 gold coins. "If MrMind manages to get profit from it without squeezing newbies or scamming he truly deserves the title of MrMind." (Lorck 2005).

I added a further explanation.

You may find this hard to believe, but I do manage to make a profit, along with everyone else who is involved in the ring making process. I have no need for scamming, and I do not cheat out noobies for their labor. It takes a very simple system of suppliers, all of whom are paid fabulously. Of course, I won't tell you how this works. (Mr.Mind 2005)

Another player added his perspective, describing Richery's low prices as a problem that threatens the stability of the game's markets and a strategy that makes the guild look bad. He concluded, "Mr.Mind—I think I realize why so many have disliked RICH and you for so long. ... Personally, I think the market needs to be fair and reasonable for all." (Arnieman 2005).

I restated my position. "The real problem here is that people will nearly always buy from whoever offers the lowest price." I challenged the other players to solve that problem and gave them my own conclusion. "In a game like this, where there is no difference in quality created, you [can only compete by offering better prices.]" I sarcastically suggested that if they wanted to take me out of the market, then they could buy me out of the market (Mr.Mind 2005).

They were not amused. "Yes, always the most effective tactic of bad businessmen—blame the consumer. ... The consumer is not responsible for your price-setting—YOU are." (Arnieman 2005).

Their point was irrelevant, but they were partially right. Yes, I set the prices that I wanted, and part of the purpose behind my prices was to push everyone else out of the market. But I set the prices based on what the customer was willing to pay. The conversation fizzled; the crafting strike broke apart in the forums before it even began, and most people blamed RICH because RICH refused to join their team. I was happy to take the credit, because every player who complained that they couldn't make money was just another message that made me proud of my guild's achievements. RICH, a guild that everyone once dismissed, graduated from a startup just trying to survive into a mega-corporation that crushes its competition. And it still hadn't reached the peak.

The Economics (Boycott)

The bigger RICH became, the more its advantage grew. The economies of scale that RICH was using for production was improved by its process of using Richery to sell products. RICH was now a well-known monopoly that could influence market prices in such a severe way that it became a popular target for everyone who could not compete. Their solution was a combination of LochnessLobster's cartel and Ember's boycott. They wanted to fix prices and also prevent RICH from spoiling the movement.

Neither plan had any chance of being successful. Bringing attention to RICH prices was free advertising for RICH sales. By bringing attention to their strike, they were also helping me get more business. The "bad" reputation as a low-cost provider made me unpopular with producers but extremely popular with consumers. The threats of boycotting were also ineffective, because the market's consumers cared about price more than principles. RICH was entrenched with a market power that could not be countered; as long as the difference between RICH prices and market prices were more than how much buyers were willing to pay to avoid RICH, then RICH would always be their first choice.

Some of these descriptions match the criticisms directed at Wal-Mart. Throughout its history, the company has been accused of driving down prices, consolidating industries, and crushing smaller competitors. Wal-Mart customers have proven that they care more about paying a lower price than any potential negatives that come from the way

Wal-Mart does business (or, if they do, maybe they just can't afford to pay more). This is why threats to boycott Wal-Mart have been ineffective. The company is simply too large to be forced into changing its business model based on a boycott. It's an expansion of the comparison between Wal-Mart and RICH that goes far beyond low prices. RICH was not only dragging prices lower; it was also wiping out smaller competitors and permanently changing the composition of the game's markets. Wal-Mart led the rise of the "big box" retailers that includes major corporations such as Target, Kroger, and Home Depot. RICH led the rise of the "undercutting" trade bots in EL, a group that began to follow RICH into high-volume, low-price territory (Fishman 2007; Walton and Huey 1993; Dubner 2016).

CHAPTER 12

Market War III

Market War II was a cold war, but it was a preview of the pressure building up to Market War III. Players were obviously boiling with contempt about the way RICH was manipulating the market and forcing others to lose money. The only thing they could do to compete was to try selling items that RICH did not sell, or try to copy the RICH guild methods. They couldn't copy the methods, but they could move to other markets. There was only one place left to hide.

RICH avoided the high-end level of the market. Anything that required an enriched fire essence was kept in the guild storage for guild members to borrow, and RICH would rarely sell those items. But the stockpile of enriched essences had become so large that I could not resist the temptation to use them as a weapon in the war against the market. RICH had already squeezed everyone out of every other manufacturing market. The only thing left that still made a significant amount of money was the best and most expensive manufacturable sword, the titanium serpent sword. These swords commanded a price of somewhere between 7,000 and 10,000 gold coins. Or, they did, until I set Richery's price to an insultingly low 1,000 gold coins.

RICH was not actually making money selling serpent swords for 1,000 gold coins. Even for RICH, it cost a minimum of 6,000 gold coins to make them. But this was not about making money. The purpose was to fix the price. I wanted to make the market believe that serpent swords were only worth 1,000 gold coins. If I made the price stick, then people might refuse to pay anything more, because players would know that RICH sells for 1,000. Then I could sell a few swords at a time and still keep everyone else out of the market. I was squeezing out the last thing that offered a healthy profit, and there was nothing that anyone could do to stop me. But they still tried.

On November 1, 2005, the EL forums erupted into a virtual riot when the EL player mauriciom called for a "market revolution." (mauriciom 2005). In his eyes, manufacturing prices were too low, and the manufacturers had to do something about it. Their solution was another strike. While this discussion was short and civil, other parts of the forums slowly began flaming against RICH, and the world inside the game was in turmoil. The "strike" was unlike any other that had been tried before. It started with manufacturers and spread to the crafting market. LochnessLobster and DrMabuse, the leaders of the previous market strikes, both demanded an embargo against RICH.

After a few weeks, the game's producers were starting to see that their efforts would not be enough. This time, for the strike to be successful at permanently raising prices, the strikers needed to eliminate their undercutting competition. They needed to neutralize The RICH Effect. One supportive player threw out an idea on how to do it: "You show those RICH members, DrMabuse. I say you go buy everything Richery has in stock to teach them a lesson they won't soon forget." (llsardonicll 2005). Inside the game, the strikers decided to go for it.[1]

Their primary target was Richery. The obvious source of their anger was his new serpent swords, but everything he sold was listed at an offensive price. No one could make any money with Richery in the market. But they could not kill Richery, and his prices were impossible to beat. This time, they came up with a different plan. The manufacturing and crafting specialists pooled their money. Instead of competing or leaving the market, their goal was to buy him out of the market. They wanted to buy everything he had until there was nothing left. Without Richery in the market, The RICH Effect would end, and the game's prices would return to normal.

It was a flawed strategy. RICH was excited to have their business. The market strikers paid Richery hundreds of thousands of gold coins. They were buying faster than RICH had ever tried to sell. Richery's store was emptied and restocked, and emptied and restocked, over and over again. His pile of gold coins just kept growing.

---

[1] There is no record of exactly which players decided to go along with this idea. I do not believe that LochnessLobster or DrMabuse were involved.

Then the unthinkable happened. The strikers ran out of money.

When it became clear that they could not buy Richery's entire stock of inventory, they panicked and tried to resell what they bought. But this flooded the market. There were no more buyers! Their extra buying transformed into massive selling. The manufacturing market crashed. The crafting market crashed. And, as a consequence of this process, *the RICH guild became even richer*. RICH even managed to buy back some of the items at the bottom of the market's crash.

I was unable to hold the serpent sword price at 1,000 gold coins over the long term, but the price settled at 5,000 gold coins, significantly lower than before, and the failed market revolution essentially ended the market wars forever. The strikers went bankrupt, and I took the credit. RICH, with less than 10 percent of the game's population, was invincible. It was the most powerful market force in Eternal Lands (EL). The intense hatred that was directed at RICH was actually making the guild stronger, and my position as the face of the guild made me the most infamous player in EL. RICH and I were infamous and evil, perhaps, but only in the eyes of the competitors, not in the eyes of the customers, and certainly not in the eyes of the RICH guild members. But I played the part. I owned the reputation that RICH earned, and I let the world of EL know that nobody could beat me.

The Economics (Anti-Competitive Behavior)

The decision to sell titanium serpent swords for 1,000 gold coins, when they cost 6,000 gold coins to make, is an obvious case of anti-competitive behavior, sometimes called an abuse of market power. RICH was trying to enhance its own market power by selling below its own cost. This is a specific kind of predatory pricing called *price dumping*. Price dumping is when a company sells its products for a loss to force competitors out of business. It is almost always illegal in the real world, but EL didn't have any rules against it. This adds a layer to how RICH can be described. RICH became an *unregulated* natural monopoly that abused its market power by intentionally losing money to drive out competitors. In a larger perspective, the market wars were an incredible and unique display of economics in action, and Market War III was the most interesting. Instead of just forming a cartel and trying to reduce the market supply—a strategy that was proven to be ineffective—they tried to artificially raise the prices by increasing the demand in the market. Market War III was actually an attempt to "corner" the market by taking all of the supply out of the market. Both of these EL descriptions have connections to real-world events.

There are not many examples of price dumping in the real world, but there is one famous case of a monopoly company abusing its market power. The case comes from a 1999 court ruling that declared Microsoft a monopoly that was abusing its market power. The issue was that Microsoft had the dominant position in the market for computer operating systems, and it used that market position to make it more difficult for Netscape and other rivals to compete with its Internet Explorer web browser. At the time, most people could only connect to the Internet using a dial-up connection, and they would only be able to use the service that was already on their computer. Since almost every computer had a Microsoft operating system (almost everyone used Windows), Microsoft could guide their customers away from their competitors' Internet services. This is not as much of an issue today because people can access the Internet through their phones, a market that Microsoft does not control. The new leader is Google. Google has a dominant position in the phone operating system market (as Android) and the Internet search market, and Google is now the one earning the attention of antitrust regulators (Fitzpatrick 2014).

Market corners are also rare in the real world. But one of the most fascinating cases of an attempted market corner comes from the 1970s, when the Hunt brothers, two of the richest people in the world at the time, attempted to corner the market for silver. After buying almost 9 percent of the world's entire supply of silver in 1974, the brothers doubled down in 1979, purchasing contracts that could have given them control of an estimated 77 percent of all the world's privately held silver. In just 1 year, the price of silver went from $16 per ounce in 1979 to over $50 an ounce in 1980. Then, after the trading exchanges changed the rules, the Hunt brothers were forced to sell their holdings; with no one willing to buy, the silver market collapsed, falling to $11 an ounce within 10 weeks of its $50 all-time high. The Hunt brothers ended up declaring bankruptcy (Iskyan 2016; Christopher 2016).

It's a fundamental rule of economics that when demand goes up, price will go up. By this rule, the attempt to corner the market in EL *should* have worked (in the real world it *almost* worked). If RICH had been selling every item for a loss, and if the group of buyers had more money than RICH had items, then RICH would have been driven out of business. But RICH was too big.

Even if there was enough money to buy RICH out of the market, the shift in demand would not last very long. Other than the serpent swords, RICH was making money on every sale. And RICH would have used this extra money to help its members level up in crafting or manufacturing. I was already doing this myself. I would borrow gold from the guild to buy iron and steel bars, make weapons and armor, sell the weapons and armor, and then harvest lilacs to make up the difference. Spreading this wealth through the bank of Richery would have quickly replenished the RICH supply of items.

Beyond RICH, the players who bought items from RICH were not permanent buyers, and they would have to try to resell everything eventually. It was an attempt at arbitrage that could not work, because the market prices that existed before RICH were no longer the real market prices. The market had accepted the RICH prices as the new market prices, and there was nothing that anyone could do to bring things back to "normal." RICH won the market wars.

The manufacturing and crafting specialists certainly had a good reason to be angry with me. Their profits were all dragged deep into the negatives, and their businesses would never recover from bombs I dropped in the market. But they might have been mistaken. When players in the game calculated their profits, they took it as a function of market price minus market cost, and they used a form called *economic profits*. It's a little different from the more common measure of accounting profit, but it's actually a more appropriate picture of the real world. Cost in these cases was based on opportunity cost, which includes implicit costs (what you don't directly pay for), and explicit costs (what you spend), while considering the next-best alternatives. What this means is that most players were not actually buying their raw materials. Instead, they were harvesting everything themselves and adding up the gold coins they would have made from selling their raw materials to the NPC. This was the opportunity cost they were giving up to produce their items. Economic profits consider the opportunity cost of your alternatives, while accounting profits only include what you actually spend. This was all fine so far, but they were not counting all of their benefits.

In EL, as we've already seen, an individual player could choose to reach for gold coins or experience points, and every player valued their progress differently. The economic choice for most players was how to maximize their total value of both gold coins and experience compared to how much time they had available. Every item gave a specific amount of experience points. Those experience points represented another form of compensation, and the items that paid the most experience points were the ones that received the most attention. Selling at a loss, when the value of experience was added, was rational. And since it was relatively easy to figure out which items paid the most experience at the lowest cost, the supply of those items ballooned out of control. In the end, the market accounted for the value of experience points by showing a lower price. This is why so many producers continued to participate in the market while complaining that they could not make money. Sometimes they made money, but they were still benefitting even when they sold at a loss; if they weren't benefitting, then they would have started doing something else. This idea was explained perfectly by one player's response to the market revolution:

> If you're not making money at what you're doing, DO SOME-THING ELSE. ... If you're doing it for [experience points], isn't that alone enough? If you're saying 'no' to that statement, then ask yourself, *what* are you **really** more interested in... the [gold coins], or the leveling? (Phenic 2005)

It was a message that most players ignored, and it was the open secret that RICH exploited. For RICH, the experience points were enough. And if we assume that a player was willing to give up the gold coins, and just take experience points, we could figure out how much they would be "paying" for every experience point. I never performed this analysis while I played the game; it was intuitive and obvious that players liked leveling up, so there must be some value to leveling up. It was also apparent that the alchemy skill, which used more mass production than the other skills, was the most popular way for new players to boost themselves in the game. But now I have the numbers to back up my intuition. Assuming players were willing to produce items for the experience points alone, and sell them for zero gold coins, I found the average price they would have been "paying" for each experience point, shown in Table 12.1.

Table 12.1 The value of experience

Average gold coin price of one experience point by skill	
Alchemy	0.19 gold coins
Crafting	1.29 gold coins
Manufacturing (excluding outliers)	2.56 gold coins

Alchemy, the most popular skill for new players, was also the cheapest skill to advance, with an average price of just 0.19 gold coins *(in other words, a player could "buy" 1 Alchemy experience point by "spending" 0.19 of a gold coin on materials)*. The price of experience for the two "final step" skills of crafting and manufacturing were significantly higher, at 1.29 and 2.56, respectively. New players could level up faster by focusing on the cheaper alchemy experience, and RICH was mostly made up of new players.

In the end, what the strikers always failed to understand was that RICH was not undercutting its competitors just to be annoying (although that was one of its goals). Because of the value of experience, every sale, even with RICH prices, was still a profitable one (except for the serpent swords). RICH was not just being hostile. RICH was also making an extraordinary amount of money.

PART IV

The Game Changes

CHAPTER 13

Cooldown

After months of players complaining about the balance of the game's economy, Entropy finally responded with a major structural change. His plan was, in essence, to simply make it more difficult to manufacture. First introduced on December 8, 2005, he called the idea "cooldown." In theory, it didn't sound like a bad idea. Under the original system, players ate food to get the energy they needed to make stuff, and there was no limit to how fast they could eat the food. The new system added a "cooldown timer" to each different type of food, limiting how fast the player could eat and therefore limiting how fast they could produce. More expensive foods had a faster cooldown, and cheaper foods had a slower cooldown. Assuming everyone chose the cheaper foods, then production would slow down, supply would decrease, and prices would increase.

Before cooldown, the most popular foods were fruits and vegetables. They could both be harvested in convenient places, usually gardens, and a single load of over 200 fruits or vegetables could fuel an entire guild party for several hours. The addition of a cooldown timer brought in a new standard.

An obscure potion, one that nobody ever used, called the potion of feasting, became the favorite choice among manufacturers. When the cooldown timers were compared with the amount of food provided, the advantage was easy to see. The challenge for the players was that the potion of feasting was not easy to produce, and the only other way to get it was to walk all the way across the massive White Stone forest, to an NPC in the White Stone City, who sold the potions for 12 gold coins each. It was a long and tedious trek of more than 15 minutes, just to find a source of food, and it still cost gold coins to buy the food! At least the players could buy as many as they needed.

Even with a long walk to buy the potion of feasting, and a type of food that costs actual gold coins, the comparison was simple. The potion of feasting was a much better option (there was only one cooldown timer, and any food that was eaten set the cooldown timer for *all* other foods until the timer expired, so a player could not have separate cooldown timers going for each individual food), shown in Table 13.1.

Table 13.1 **The price of cooldown**

Type of food	Increase in food level	Cooldown (seconds)	Cost (gold coins)
Bread	10	20	1
Vegetables	15	50	0
Fruits	20	60	0
Cooked meat	25	14	5
Potion of feasting	50	10	12

It was a controversial addition to the game because cooldown affected almost every consumable item, and a few power players were so outraged about changing their strategies that they decided to quit EL. No one inside RICH quit over cooldown, but the adjustment was painful.

Most of the players in the game, including most of the players in RICH, switched to the potion of feasting, but others were cautious about the overall benefits. I still tried to make it work. Fruits were cheaper, but they were much slower. A test was not necessary, because I could have done the math, but I stubbornly refused to pay gold coins for my food. But while I sat on the floor in a guild party waiting for a slow cooldown time, I saw that everyone around me was producing much faster. It was only a few seconds of difference, but when thousands of items are being produced, the seconds added up to a painfully long time. The high-level guild leaders were right. Sometimes it's better to pay more. More expensive foods allowed faster production, and faster production meant faster gold coins and faster levels.

In the end, even when the new cost calculations included cooldown costs, RICH still maintained the best prices. Manufacturing did not get much slower, but it did become more expensive, and the new cooldown system didn't do anything to take away the advantage that RICH had already built up.

The Economics (Opportunity Cost)

Shifting the numbers from Table 13.1 shows how the seconds added up. If we adjust each type of food to provide the same overall increase of 300, the effect of the cooldown timer is magnified, shown in Table 13.2.

Table 13.2 The adjusted price of cooldown

Type of food	Total increase in food level	Amount of food eaten	Total cooldown (seconds)	Total cost (gold coins)
Bread	300	30	600	30
Vegetables	300	20	1,000	0
Fruits	300	15	900	0
Cooked meat	300	12	168	60
Potion of feasting	300	6	60	72

The new question becomes whether 840 seconds of a player's time (the difference between 15 fruits cooldown and 6 potion of feasting cooldown) is worth 72 gold coins. Or, to make it more understandable, whether it was worth paying about 300 gold coins to save an hour of cooldown time. Ignoring the time spent walking to the potion seller, which could be spread out over hundreds of potions, the answer was so obvious that nobody needed to do the math: It only took 6 potion of feasting to get the same amount of food as 15 fruits or 20 vegetables, and the cooldown was more than 10 times faster. The effect on manufacturing was not what Entropy had intended.[1] The fastest cooldown

---

[1]There were other consequences for the fighting system, but that's beyond the scope of our analysis here.

became the standard, and the cost of the most expensive food was added to everyone's costs.

Cooldown did not change the market prices. Prices continued to be under pressure from The RICH Effect, and Entropy had raised the costs. It was an experiment that demonstrated how much players valued their time. Fruits were suitable for everyday gameplay and extremely small projects, but the potion of feasting was always used for mass manufacturing.

In the real world, thinking about opportunity costs in this kind of cost-benefit analysis can be valuable, and time management can be understood more clearly when the seconds are added up over a long period of time. Everything takes time, or money, or both, and considering all of the options against a common benefit or expense can make the comparison much easier. An entertaining example of how time can be compared to money is extreme couponing. Extreme couponers spend their time searching for coupons, comparing deals, and planning their shopping trips, with a goal to save as much money as possible. But while it seems like saving, the time spent gathering these coupons and planning for a shopping trip is not considered. The extreme couponers would almost always be better off taking a job and using the money from that job to pay full price (Mateer 2018).

CHAPTER 14

The Emerald Valley Trade Route

While he was developing the cooldown system, Entropy was also building what would become the most anticipated and most successful addition to the game. In this update, the land mass of the game was more than doubled, new monsters were added, and several more items were introduced. It was an entirely new continent that he named Irilion. The players called it "c2" ("c1" was Seridia, the first continent).

When the new continent was introduced into the game, it was still off-limits until the development could be completed. It was technically finished, but nobody was allowed to see it until every piece was polished and perfected. And to keep everyone out, the game's moderators guarded the boat to the continent's only entrance; anyone caught attempting to sneak on to the boat to Irilion would be sent to the Underworld.

It was still worth making an attempt. If RICH could get inside c2 before anyone else, then RICH could find the most efficient production routes inside the continent before anyone else even had a chance to look for them. This would allow RICH to maintain its lead in the market. So RICH tried to get in.

After a few failed attempts, two RICH guild members finally slipped through the moderator security and sailed to c2. When they arrived in Irilion, they split up and spent days walking through the continent. The pictures and reports that these RICH players sent in about Irilion mines and storage areas were astonishing. The distance between important resources was much shorter than Seridia. The ability to hide bags of resources would make large guild projects easier. The new monsters and secret locations made it even more appealing. It was all great for the guild, and it would be valuable information for the move to c2. However, even if most of the guild moved to c2, I would stay in Seridia, because I could bring in new guild members better than anyone else, and I would never find any new players in Irilion.

There was one more thing that I didn't say. It was a secret that I kept for a long time after I quit playing the game. No one in the game knew about it. No one in the guild knew about it. I didn't even tell the Guild Council. The secret was that RICH was so well-connected that the guild *already had a guy on the inside of the game*. RICH had the power to make changes in the game that would benefit RICH.

The development team and the moderation team were both made up of players who volunteered to help make the game better. This was unusual among MMOs, but it gave the players a voice in the future of the game's development, and it provided Entropy with a wealth of creative programming and storytelling talent. This way of developing the game made it possible for Entropy to produce more content while keeping the game free to play, and it gave him an easier way to enforce the rules, get new ideas, and access better programming. But there was a downside that Entropy could not control. Most of the players who became part of the development team were also members of a guild. If the wrong kind of guild was trusted with development powers, the result could provide one guild with an embedded advantage.

Everyone considered RICH to be the wrong type of guild. RICH was openly aggressive with the moderators, and it advertised itself in the market as a guild that was built to break the game. Anyone inside the guild who applied to be a developer or a moderator was required to drop their RICH tag and promise to be neutral. Most of the players who were offered these powers were willing to leave RICH and remain friendly while keeping their involvement fair, but there was one who carried their loyalty to the extreme. Eon_Schmidt, the Brazilian programmer, was one former RICH member whose commitment to RICH went beyond friendship.

Eon_Schmidt left the guild to become part of the design team for Irilion. His job was to build what was called the Emerald Valley Trade Route (EVTR). His responsibility was to make a piece of the world that would be nice to look at but also useful for every player; it had to be both beautiful and unbiased. But what Eon_Schmidt promised and what he planned were very different things. The EVTR would be well-designed, but it would be built with a bias towards RICH.

When the development for Irilion was still in the planning stages, Eon_Schmidt told me about his hidden project. He was working on a secret mine. The mine would have everything that RICH needed to make iron and steel bars. The guild could manufacture weapons and armor without leaving the mine. No one else would be able to find it unless a RICH member leaked its location, and no one else would be able to compete with an output that did not require any walking. It was an advantage that RICH did not need, and it was extremely unfair. But, since this was just a game, I was willing to see how far it could go.

Irilion's opening was flawless. The EVTR was everything that Eon_Schmidt promised. The map was covered in green trees and green grass, but I only cared about the secret mine. It was hidden under the cellar beneath the local tavern. Inside this cellar was a stack of wine bottles, and if a player pushed the right one, they'd find the RICH mine. Inside this hidden mine, designed by a former RICH member just for the benefit of RICH, was a spot where players could harvest coal and iron ore without even standing up; players could make iron and steel bars without walking halfway across a continent. Even in the case of the closest mines in Seridia, it took more than 5 minutes to walk from one mine to another or from a mine to a storage. The secret RICH mine could do it all without forcing anyone to move, and the new features of the game allowed players to hide massive bags of resources inside the mine without looking for a storage. RICH was already the most powerful guild in the market, but this mine would allow RICH to completely break the game. Eon_Schmidt was proof that the guild could undermine even the highest levels of the game's organization. And although the mine was not hardcoded to only be accessible by RICH, it was a secret that only RICH would know, and nobody would find it unless RICH told the others where to look.

The Economics (Regulatory Capture)

Good gamers game the game, but the creation of the RICH mine was beyond gaming the game. It was like playing a game of Monopoly and having the banker give some extra money to their favorite player. It was actually even worse than that. Because RICH was already the most efficient producer with the biggest pile of gold coins, it was more like having the banker give some extra money to the player who already owns the most property and has the most money. That is entirely unfair. So why accept an unfair advantage, and why not leave it out of the story? It's worth recognizing because it fits the type of evil empire that my character was building, and it is important to include because this type of market failure is far too common in the real world. This is an issue that must be identified in the real world.

Moral questions aside, the RICH mine represented a serious economic problem.[1] Eon_Schmidt joining the Eternal Lands (EL) development team was a pure example of *regulatory capture*. Regulatory capture is what happens when an organization created to keep a market fair is taken over by the firms that it's meant to regulate, and it ends up advancing their interests over the society's interests. As a way of preventing potential regulatory capture, the game's developers were required to promise that they would not help RICH. But there was no way to be certain that these developers would keep their promise. Eon_Schmidt was supposed to be neutral, but he was helping RICH at the expense of everyone else.

The most obvious real-world example of regulatory capture is the appointment of Ajit Pai, a former Verizon Wireless lawyer, as the Chairman of the Federal Communications Commission (FCC) in 2017.[2] The FCC regulates telecommunications and media companies, and it has historically supported a set of rules called Network Neutrality. Network Neutrality, in short, is the idea that Internet Service Providers (ISPs), such as Comcast and Verizon, should treat all Internet users equally. This means two things:

- An ISP cannot slow down or block the connection to a website, and it cannot favor one Internet business over another.
- Internet companies, like Facebook, Amazon, Google, or Netflix, cannot pay an ISP extra money to give their own service an advantage.

---

[1] If we think about the basic inputs of land, labor, capital, and entrepreneurship, the mine was also a way for RICH to get cheaper land.

[2] There are many other potential examples, but this is one of the most well-known, and the easiest to understand.

Within a year of the FCC's leadership change, the agency's support for Network Neutrality was formally changed; the FCC voted to roll back a regulation called "Title II" that required ISPs to follow Network Neutrality rules. It still remains to be seen how the ISPs' behavior might change, and what the government might do to formalize these rules into laws, but this rule change allows ISPs to favor some Internet users over others for any reason that they choose. It's an ISP victory made possible by an industry insider (Wheeler 2017).[3]

This process of trying to get an insider's influence is called *rent seeking*. Rent seeking is what happens when a company uses its resources to influence an unfair regulatory advantage instead of actually competing. It usually comes in the form of lobbying for protection against competitors. This can be special tax benefits, subsidies, or laws against market competition. In EL, it was actually the RICH competitors who lobbied for changes to offset The RICH Effect. RICH, as a group, did not actively seek an unfair advantage. But Eon_Schmidt, as an extension of RICH, represents rent seeking.

Rent seeking in the real world is incredibly common. Almost every major company spends some money on lobbying efforts. These efforts are not always bad or unfair, because they can be used to provide important information on complex ideas. But when they are used to create unnecessary artificial barriers to entry for a market (meaning, a barrier that entrenches market power rather than ensuring a product's basic quality), that perfectly fits the definition of rent seeking.

---

[3]There are always more nuances to these controversial issues. The important point to understand is the process of recognizing who is making a decision, what their incentives or loyalties might be, and whether that matches the observation of a neutral third party and the intended goals of the organization.

CHAPTER 15

Hydrogenium

After introducing Irilion, Entropy added a series of updates designed to encourage players to visit the second continent. The first was a group of NPCs that he called guild NPCs. They were announced in January 2006 but added as part of the new features for c2. A guild NPC functioned in almost exactly the same way as a regular NPC—it worked as a shop that would buy and sell items—but this NPC would be controlled by a guild. The guild NPC was also similar to a trade bot. It could only sell what the owner gave it to sell, and the gold from every sale would go to the guild. There were three main differences between a trade bot and a guild NPC:

- A guild NPC had a warehouse-like amount of storage.
- It could not advertise for itself.
- It was paid for with gold coins instead of real dollars.

Overall, these features were nice, but the most attractive benefit was that all of the guild NPCs would be in Irilion. RICH needed to have one.

The guild NPCs were put up for auction. Whichever guild placed the final bid would pay the monthly rent of their winning bid. After an intense contest, RICH won the bid for a new female guild NPC named Dacia, with a rental rate of 35,000 gold coins per month. Dacia would become a new base of operations for RICH, and the guild's only major entry to c2.

Dacia was more than a guild shop. She also replaced Richery's previous role as guild storage, something the guild had been missing since Richery became the guild's trade bot. She could hold an almost unlimited amount of items that guild members could store and share with each other. She could keep the guild's gold, materials, and finished products all in one place.

Her shop helped the guild become more organized, and my involvement was no longer necessary. Dacia could keep everything that I might have held for the guild, and the Guild Council members—the only other players who had access to Dacia's warehouse—were all smart enough to run the guild without me. I didn't even need to make any decisions. My only role, at this point, was to be the one who takes the credit for the RICH guild's reputation. It was time to consider leaving the game. I would be graduating from high school soon and giving up video games to focus on college.

As I prepared for my exit from the game, I made a statement in the EL forums, posted on April 27, 2006, announcing my retirement and calling myself the master of the EL economy.[1] Then I moved on to securing the internal stability of the guild. Since the only people who actually wanted to be the guild master were not a good fit, I decided to set Richery as the guild master. I split each guild leader's responsibility. The guild was big enough to run by committee, and Richery could serve as the administrator bot that enabled the guild to vote on what to do. I hoped that it would relax any tension about who held which powers.

While this transition was in progress, Entropy introduced another new feature. It was a new metal ore that he called hydrogenium ore. The new metal ore used steel two-edged swords to harvest (each sword was destroyed while harvesting for a chance to get one ore). It was located in an area somewhere in c2 that required passing through a lava field on a narrow path where other players could attack. It would be used to produce hydrogenium bars, which were metal bars made for manufacturing special new swords. Entropy's reasons for creating these conditions were theoretically valid (Privantu 2006):

1. To reduce the oversupply of steel two-edged swords.
2. To prevent players from mass producing hydrogenium bars. This was intended to set a minimum price for the new weapons and armors by keeping them rare.
3. To make harvesting more dangerous.
4. To encourage players to visit Irilion.
5. To encourage the merchant guilds and the fighting guilds to work together.

---

[1] See Appendix A for a review of the responses to my retirement.

These brand-new items, announced on May 14, 2006, coincided with the RICH guild's restructuring. I saw it as an opportunity to unify the guild; one more major project to set the new leadership's standards. And when the plans for producing these new swords were ready, I left the game for what I thought would be forever.[2] As I was on my way out, I made some suggestions for balancing the game's economy, but I could not offer any quick fixes. Then I left for college.

The Economics (Principal/Agent Problem)

Dacia was a mark of the progress that RICH made. The guild had grown from struggling to secure an initial 30,000 gold coin investment to easily renting a warehouse-like storage for 35,000 gold coins every month. It went from one highly qualified guild leader to more than 25, with a peak membership of more than 200 members.[3] The guild was embedded into the game's markets, development team, and even its moderation team.[4] As an economic summary:

1. RICH found a way to get cheaper labor.
2. This cheaper labor created economies of scale for the guild.
3. The economies of scale were an advantage that led to monopoly market power.
4. RICH used its market power for predatory pricing and regulatory capture.

---

[2]When I left EL in 2006, I was listed as the 10th highest level manufacturer (trollson was ranked 9th and eventually rose to 8th), 37th in crafting (SiKiK was 30th and eventually rose to 8th, passing DrMabuse on the way up), and 18th in summoning. No other player made the top 50 in all three of those skills. I was also ranked 58 in harvesting, 152 in alchemy, 190 in potions, and 133 overall (a high ranking for a character that did not work on fighting skills). I had no desire to chase numbers on a leaderboard, but the continued rise of trollson and SiKiK is more evidence that the RICH methods could be successful without my direction.

[3]I began purging inactive members after RICH became the largest guild in the game. Excluding this practice makes the real number of total members nearly impossible to count, and the archived record has a gap of more than 4 months during this time period.

[4]Although none of the moderators openly favored RICH, the moderators who were former RICH members often gently advised the guild to back off when a harsh punishment was being considered.

This complete combination is unlikely to be found in a modern business, but it was a common feature of the Gilded Age of the Robber Barons in the late 1800s and early 1900s, before the spread of labor protection and antitrust enforcement. Modern monopolies usually come from different sources and rarely use predatory pricing, but regulatory capture continues to be a serious issue.

Moving on from what RICH became, considering the potential challenges involved when founders retire from the companies that they built, what happens when the guild master leaves? There were RICH guild members who lusted after the guild's wealth, but I rejected their offers to take over as guild master. Not only were they not capable, they were also not trustworthy. It was a dilemma that economists call the *principal/agent problem*. This is what happens when there is someone who makes decisions on behalf of other people, but also has powerful incentives to put their own interests first. In the real world, this would be a corporate management team in charge of shareholders' money. There are many examples from the 2008 financial crisis of bank managers making bad loans; they got paid to make the loans without any questions about the quality of the loans (Lewis 2010). In RICH, it was the Guild Council controlling the guild's assets. I had to choose a new leader with enough reputational capital to be respected by the guild members, and enough human capital to keep track of the guild's operations. None of my top choices had enough time to run the guild (they all had real jobs with demanding schedules), but trollson became the temporary guild master until Richery's administrator code could be finished.

The new hydrogenium materials were an interesting experiment for Entropy and a big risk for RICH. They were primarily intended to prop up the market for steel two-edged swords. It was a creative way of adding a potential price control without using an NPC. Instead of simply setting a price floor, Entropy was adding to the demand for steel two-edged swords. And when demand goes up, price goes up. So, while the idea was weird, it was an economically sound strategy for that particular market. The question was: When the supply of steel two-edged swords is completely transformed into a supply for hydrogenium, what happens to the market for hydrogenium? This is what is called a *second-order effect*. The direct, first-order effect would be fewer steel two-edged swords.

What comes next is the second-order effect, which will be fully explained in the next chapter.

For RICH and the other producers, the race to hydrogenium was a gold rush. Whoever got there first would own the initial market and get the highest profits (they would have the first-mover advantage); anyone coming later would be left with whatever they could get as the prices settled into a lower level. I believed that RICH had the best ability to be the first one to the market, but I only stayed long enough to help develop the plan. Everything else would be left to the players I trusted and the process I had proven.

CHAPTER 16

Broken and Rebuilt

When I first walked away from the game, I was completely certain that I would never return. I had no reason to come back to a game that I already beat, and I could still e-mail anyone I knew who played the game with me. Through my first year of college, I never even bothered to check the progress of the guild. I barely ever thought about EL. I fully moved on with my life and focused on school.

Nine months after I left the game, while I was thinking about what to do with a slow summer break, I decided to come back and see how things had changed. I still didn't want to play, but I was curious about how much my guild's wealth had grown. I believed that the systematic advantage I had built could never be beaten. And if I had never logged in again, then I never would have learned how the story actually ends. I could have stopped there, with RICH at the top of everything, but I have to be true to what really happened.

When I signed back into EL in May 2007, I expected to see a busy RICH guild that I could admire with pride, but what I found was depressing. RICH was a guild on life support. The guild chat was silent, and my message screen was empty. There weren't any RICH members anywhere in the game at all. RICH was once the biggest and most powerful guild in the game, but something had blown it up.

After about 2 hours, I finally found someone who could tell me the whole story. What they told me was not good news. RICH no longer had any market power. The guild had splintered into separate groups who disagreed on how it should be managed, with most of them ultimately choosing to go out on their own. What was once RICH—"The Wal-Mart of Eternal Lands"—was now five "mini-RICH" guilds made up of former RICH members. It was a small group of large, powerful producers, and RICH itself was not among this group. RICH was still officially the fourth largest guild in the game, with 139 total members, but almost all of them were inactive. It also had a little more than 250,000 gold coins, but it was much less than what the guild had before I left, and RICH had been bleeding money for months with no hope for a reversal. I had never considered that RICH could ever be in such bad financial shape.[1]

Although the competition from the new mini-RICH guilds probably eroded the remaining influence of RICH, it was not the market that broke the guild. It was the guild's leaders that tore the guild apart. When they disagreed, and they sometimes violently disagreed, there was no founder around to encourage a compromise and force a final decision. It became so personally offensive that most of the best members decided that they would be better off on their own. When they left, they took their experience of the guild party, their knowledge of the RICH mine, and always a few of their friends. They never took any money, but they never needed to take any money. What they took was far more valuable to the guild than gold coins. When they left, they left with their knowledge of how RICH operated and a solid base of players who were motivated to repeat the rise of another RICH. There were only about seven active RICH players remaining.

I say that these players left, but it would more accurate to say that they were driven away. The problem was that, when I retired from the game, I did not realize how easily RICH could become unstable or how much chaos one bad player could cause. Richery never became the guild master because his code was never stable enough to trust. Instead, trollson continued to be the guild master. The RICH guild was still a powerful manufacturing machine while he was the leader, but when his real life became too busy, he turned it over to SiKiK. Within 2 months after the transition, SiKiK was banned from the game. By this time, there was only one remaining member who had the time and the desire to run the guild, but it was also the one person I never wanted to be in charge. The new leader's name was TirunCollimdus, a man who most of the guild's members appropriately nicknamed "Tiruny" (tyranny).

---

[1] It is yet another mark of the guild's progress for me to consider 250,000 gold coins to be too low.

Tiruny, who thought of the guild as his "family," demanded that the guild members call him "father." I never found out why he wanted it that way, but I could understand why so many old RICH players went somewhere better. The new RICH guild was popular among other guilds—its reputation had been fully repaired, and it was no longer considered to be a threat to the market—but Tiruny had also removed everything that made RICH remarkable, and the guild's new projects had nothing to do with production. Instead, Tiruny's idea for how to make money in the game was to have the whole guild *harvest lilacs* to buy things. That was entirely the opposite of everything that RICH was created to be! It was the same thing that my brother's old guilds had demanded from him.

The more I heard about Tiruny's path to the guild master position, the more I recognized my failure in judgement. Even as I moved forward with my EL retirement, Tiruny's intimidation was already well-known; he could never admit to being wrong about anything, and *he could never stop explaining why he was never wrong.* I was aware of his short temper and long-winded tirades, but, at the time, when I asked him to leave the guild, he had the power to refuse my authority. He controlled the guild's message board, and his permission was needed to access it. He owned the connection to all of the guild's secret information and all of the guild's communications, and he knew that he had this power. When I first asked him to leave, he threatened to steal the guild's data, shut down the communications, and reveal anything he knew that might hurt the guild (including the location of the secret RICH mine). I was not interested in the months that it would take to recover the data, and I didn't want to dilute the market power that RICH had acquired, so I let it go and I let him stay. If I had known I was choosing between my data and my guild, and if I had known that keeping him around would lead to the destruction of both, then I would have dumped him right away.

I still tried. I asked another guild member to copy the guild's records. But it was not possible. Something about the way the message board was constructed made it impossible to copy quickly. Then the attempt was discovered by Tiruny, and the small amount of respect (if any) that remained between him and the other guild leaders was irreparably broken. This created a split within the RICH guild that I did not have the time to address before leaving. I naively hoped that it would heal on its own.

When I retired from the guild master position, I arranged for each guild leader to be in charge of one piece of the guild's management. I ordered Tiruny to focus on the guild's relationships with other guilds. The reason I chose him for this position was that, assuming he stayed within the boundaries of his position, there was nothing he could do to further damage the internal stability of the guild. But because I failed to remove his informal power over the guild, there was nothing anyone could do to prevent him from escalating the conflict.

Soon after I left, in the story that I pieced together from the remaining and former RICH members, Tiruny began to verbally abuse other guild leaders. The players who attempted to remove his control of the RICH message board, and anyone associated with them, were all targets of his terror. And when the internal struggle became too personal to be appropriate for a video game, they left to form their own guilds. Others, disgusted by Tiruny's attitude, with no way of avoiding his insults, simply walked away. And as the RICH guild's most important members left, Tiruny expanded his power to include their responsibilities. As the guild shrank, his personal power grew. By the time SiKiK became the guild master, there were no other active guild leaders. When SiKiK was suspiciously banned from the game, presumably for something that he said privately inside the RICH message board, Tiruny became the guild master by default.

The guild's problems, however, were a bit larger than trusting the wrong person. The manufacturing project that I organized was, while finished, still unsuccessful. The swords produced from the hydrogenium bars were never sold. My hope for the project was that it would unify the guild and stabilize the guild's long-term finances, but it did not work that way. The project made a large number of exotic swords that were introduced as new items. Being new items, I had no idea what the demand would be, or even if there would be any demand at all, and it was a huge gamble on an unknown market. I also broke the guild's number one manufacturing rule and bought most of the raw materials. My goal was to speed up the production, but that did not work either. The way it turned out, by the time RICH finished manufacturing the swords, there were no longer any buyers; RICH was not the fastest producer to reach the market. For most players, the only reason to own any of these swords was to show off their wealth, so there was very little demand. The project failed to make any money, and it was not enough to keep the guild together.

Despite all of these complications, it was not too late to rebuild the RICH guild. I knew I could bring it back if I had the chance. But I was not interested in actually playing, and Eternal Lands was not the same game that I had played before. Most of the official changes were about how the game looked, so the game's design would not affect my strategy, but the competition was much smarter. Now everyone, *even LochnessLobster*, was playing the RICH way. The market had shifted, and RICH no longer had an advantage. Everyone mass-produced, and everyone used the guild parties. RICH had been copied by so many guilds, many of them started by former RICH members, that it would be impossible to bring RICH back to the top. But I did not need to take RICH back to the top. I just wanted to see it survive.

To regain control over the guild, I had to persuade Tiruny to hand it back to me. And I had to be sensitive with my words, because, as the RICH guild's official guild master, he had the power to refuse my request. But I was lucky. When I told him that I had decided to come back to the game, he confessed that he was finding the guild difficult to manage. He unexpectedly conceded that I would always be the one in control of the guild, no matter who officially held the guild master title. He handed me the title of guild master and left RICH to start his own guild. Most of the remaining guild members went with him. The only ones left were a few strangers and some old RICH members who rarely played.

Rebuilding the guild was a challenge that I had faced before, but this time the details were different. The RICH collapse left a hole in the market that other mini-RICH guilds quickly filled, and there was too much efficient competition to win another market war. This time, I would not try to win. This time I would have to look at the market in a different way. Other guilds could copy everything they wanted, but RICH had something that no other guild in the game could copy—RICH had my network of loyal friends.

I always considered the keys to power (or at least stability) in EL as just a combination of members and money. Tiruny's terror had exhausted the guild's leadership and depleted its membership; most of them either left to form their own guilds or quit the game entirely. This meant that the first thing I had to do was refill the guild's membership. When Tiruny left, I assumed that anyone who stayed behind was more loyal to RICH than to Tiruny, so I instantly promoted them all to the Guild Council. Then I started looking outside.

I pulled out my RICH contact list and sent an e-mail to everyone I knew. The message was personalized for each contact, but, in general, it said, "It's me, Mr.Mind. I'm back in EL and I need your help. RICH is dying and I want to save it. I'm the guildmaster again." trollson was suspicious that the e-mail came from an imposter, but after confirming that it was me, he decided to be more active in EL. trollson came back to the game. His colleague Lunksnark came back. seanodonnell came back. SiKiK persuaded Entropy to unban him so that he could come back as well. Within a week, the guild's leadership was at full strength. Within a month, another 70 active members flooded into the guild. No one else in EL could do that. No matter how much of RICH they copied, *no one* could do that. That was the real RICH advantage. It was always about keeping a strong connection to the players who loved the guild.

Now that RICH had the members to grow on its own, I needed to find the money. Using another guild project was possible, but, although I was back to playing EL like it was a full-time job, I did not want to put in that much effort. All I wanted to do was to stabilize the guild and get back to the real world. And this time I would do it in the right way. There had to be some unknown assets hiding somewhere inside the RICH warehouses. There had to be something of value that RICH still owned. I checked inside Richery's store and there was nothing there. Then I looked at the list of what was held inside Dacia's warehouse. She had piles of sulfur, leather armors, dung (yes, *dung!*), and mostly other junk. But buried in her list of materials was one item that I could still try to sell. Sitting in her storage, untouched for almost 6 months, was a stash of 50 exotic swords. They were the same swords that I had commissioned before I retired from EL. I considered all the time and all the work that had gone into producing those swords, and it was sad to see that no one had been able to sell them. That would be my first move.

I went into the market channel to check the value of the swords. The response was that an NPC would buy them for 30,000 gold coins each; Entropy had set a minimum price on the swords. Selling them at that price would be selling them for a substantial loss, but they were worth much more as gold coins than as swords. So I sold them, all of them, for a total of 1.5 million gold coins. RICH was back in business. RICH was rich again.

Everything was easy up to this point. The new members and the new money were already available, and all I had to do was find them. But one more problem persisted. Tiruny still controlled the guild's communication system, and he was still using it to make demands from RICH. And after his unreasonable demands were ignored, he followed through on the promise he had made the year before: he locked down the RICH forums; banned every RICH member; and began changing their posts to make it look like they said things that they didn't say. My patience was exhausted.

The dispute spread into the official EL forums. On July 26, 2007, using the information that I gathered from the former guild members who weathered his abuse (including a former member who was now a moderator), I outlined his record of nasty behavior in the outlaws section of the official EL message board. I did not like the way that Tiruny publicly pretended to be an honorable person while he privately tried to sabotage people, and I described how he didn't have the integrity that he claimed. It was a sensational conversation that quickly devolved into an aggressive argument. Tiruny had some supporters who claimed that they'd never seen any bad behavior, while there were others who were not surprised. Tiruny directed his fury at anyone who had the courage to doubt his authenticity. It went on for a few days until the moderators demanded a resolution and closed the topic.[2]

---

[2]The end of Tiruny's EL career is a lesson on ethics that goes far beyond the game. When another dispute against Tiruny spilled into other parts of the EL forums, he was forced to resign from his new guild after publicly attacking some of *his own guild members* who began to question his integrity (TirunCollimdus 2007). He was later banned from the game entirely for stealing his wife's character and giving all of her stuff to his new girlfriend (TirunCollimdus 2009). He also convinced his girlfriend, who was married to another man, to leave her husband and run away with him (TirunCollimdus 2009). Tiruny then came back to my outlaw topic, *three years after it was closed*, to continue arguing that he was an honorable person who was treated unfairly (TirunCollimdus 2010). But, by then, nobody cared anymore, and most people didn't even know him. After that, he disappeared from the Internet forever.

Meanwhile, RICH was allowed access to its old forums, but it abandoned the effort to save any useful information when it found that most of the guild's important records were unrecoverable. The guild started over with a new data collection effort in a new forum managed by Lunksnark and trollson. The last piece of my recovery plan was finally in place. It was time to leave the game for good.

The Economics (Monopoly to Oligopoly)

When the RICH guild's monopoly broke apart, the market did not go back to the way it was before RICH. The market became something else. Before RICH, the market was a large group of smaller producers (a perfectly competitive market). After the RICH monopoly broke apart, the market became an *oligopoly*. An oligopoly market is one with a small number of large, powerful producers. There are many examples of oligopolies in the real world, but we'll focus on two examples that match the transformation of the EL markets. These are industries where a monopoly producer was broken into smaller pieces that still controlled the market: Standard Oil and AT&T.

Standard Oil, a model of vertical integration, with operations that covered drilling, refining, transportation, and sale of oil, was a giant of the Gilded Age that controlled over 90 percent of the United States' oil production by 1900. In 1911, the company was accused of abusing its monopoly market power. By the power of the Sherman Antitrust Act of 1890, it was forced to split into 34 smaller companies. Over the past 100 years, many of those companies merged back together, and they still exist as Chevron and ExxonMobil. What was once a monopoly broke up and reformed into an oligopoly (Economist 1999; Chernow 1998; Desjardins 2017).

The story of AT&T is similar to Standard Oil. Unlike Standard Oil, AT&T's telephone monopoly was permitted and regulated by the

---

This unbelievable story was summarized to me in a personal communication with bagjumper on January 21, 2017 and confirmed through primary sources in the Eternal Lands Official Forums. It reinforces the importance of choosing the right people for a leadership team.

government for almost 100 years. But it was also forced to break up, by the same Sherman Antitrust Act, in 1982 (the breakup became official in 1984). AT&T became seven different "Baby Bell" companies. Over time, these companies also merged back together, and they now survive as Verizon Communications and AT&T Inc. It was another monopoly market that split up and rebuilt itself as an oligopoly (Pagliery 2014; Investopedia 2018).

The RICH story is a little different. RICH was not regulated, so it was never at risk of a forced breakup. Instead, RICH broke apart on its own without any outside intervention.[3] The risk of the principal-agent problem had become a reality; bad leadership caused RICH to disintegrate, and the only thing I could do was stabilize the situation. To do that, there were two steps I had to take. The first thing I had to do was to convince some of the old members to come back. The second thing I had to do was to clean up the guild's financial situation, and that meant selling the guild's valuable swords.

When I asked for help, the former RICH members responded emphatically.[4] The fact that there were 70 players willing to come back to the guild—a number that, by itself, would have almost made a top-10 guild on its own—was a demonstration of the unique experience that the guild could provide. In economic terms, they were drawn to the reputational capital that I had promoted during my time as the guild master of RICH. And it was the guild's early investments in human capital that made it possible for these members to make immediately valuable contributions.

The guild's leftover materials were also valuable. The exotic swords that RICH had in storage were worth less than it cost the guild to produce them. However, the cost to produce them was a *sunk cost*. This means that the cost to make them had already been spent, could not be recovered, and should not be considered. Thinking about the swords as a sunk cost made it easy to see that selling them, even at a "loss," was the right thing

---

[3]If we talk about players leaving the guild in terms of the four factors of production—land, labor, capital, and entrepreneurship—the players who left the guild were taking the most valuable land (represented by their knowledge of the RICH mine), lots of labor, and the leadership (entrepreneurship) that made RICH an efficient producer.
[4]I did ask other guilds if they would merge with RICH, but none of them were interested.

to do, because the sunk costs counted as zero. It was just good luck for the guild that Entropy added an NPC with a price floor limiting how low exotic swords could sell for.

When Entropy set up a new NPC to buy his exotic swords, it was the answer to the last chapter's question about second-order effects. That question was, "When the supply of steel two-edged swords is completely transformed into a supply for hydrogenium, what happens to the market for hydrogenium?" The new hydrogenium ore successfully reduced the number of steel two-edged swords in the game. But an oversupply of steel two-edged swords became an oversupply of hydrogenium, and an over-supply of hydrogenium became an oversupply of exotic swords. As the supply kept rising, prices kept falling. It did not fix Entropy's problem. It only shifted the problem to another market, where Entropy was forced to address it directly as a second-order effect. It was an excellent experiment, but this result was always the most likely outcome. In economics, the effects of one change never end in the same market where they begin.

There are people who have made millions and billions of dollars just by seeking out and exploiting these second-order effects. The most widely reported examples are the investment firms that saw a potential housing market collapse coming before 2008. The story was brilliantly detailed in Michael Lewis' book, *The Big Short*, and the movie by the same name: These investment firms recognized that the housing market collapse would lead to problems with mortgages, and the mortgage problems would become bank problems. When the 2008 financial crisis began, they made money by betting on both mortgage problems and bank problems. It's a short and simplified explanation, but it shows the value that can come from looking for second-order effects. This value holds true even if the goal is just to avoid losing money.

CHAPTER 17

The New Eternal Lands

When I quit the game for the second time, I chose not to bring any attention to where the guild was going. I was no longer the face of RICH and I no longer had much influence on the culture of the game, so I had no need to announce another retirement. The guild's new plans would be made by a new guild master without my direction.

This time I made sure to get the transition right. I knew that I could not have the guild run by a committee, and I knew that I needed a guild master who could run a guild with intelligence and integrity. I needed someone who cared about what was best for the guild but did not consider their personal power to be important. There were a few qualified players who supported me from the very beginning—certainly seanodonnell, SiKiK, or trollson—but most of them did not want to play the game that often. I needed someone who was planning to stick around.

I took an unconventional approach to the transition, and chose Lu05, an Englishwoman in her 30s, to be the next guild master of RICH. She joined RICH while Tiruny was in charge, but she was one of the few who stayed behind to help me rebuild the guild. Her loyalty was not to me or to Tiruny. She was a true supporter of the entire guild, and she knew what she was doing. The fact that RICH briefly regained its status as the game's largest guild, and continues to sit solidly at number two, while almost every other guild has died, is proof that I made the right choice.

When the transition was complete, I made my way to the Portland beach cabin that I called my retirement home, and walked away from the EL life I left behind: murders and market wars; and the dramatic rise and fall, and rebirth, of the game's greatest power. There was no way that real life could ever compete with what this game provided. But no game, no matter what it can do, can ever be a proper substitute for real life. I

uninstalled Eternal Lands on August 13, 2007 (right before returning
to school), left a short goodbye message for the guild, and never played
again.[1]

RICH is much smaller now—both Richery and Dacia were abandoned (although Richery was later revived)—but so is the game; EL only
has a few more than 150 daily active players remaining, and there are
more trading bots than players. The RICH guild will never be what it
was before, because EL has changed. Some of these changes were directed
at the RICH strategy, and some were even influenced by RICH members, but many complaints were also ignored. The rules were amended
(the "illegal multiplay" rule that led to Richery's ban was removed). New
skills and items were added. New pictures and sounds were introduced.
The lilac bush was killed, and the secret RICH mine was emptied. But
the overall substance of the game, and the parts that I exploited, mostly
stayed the same.

Entropy continued to introduce new ores that require different swords
for harvesting. For his goal of reducing the number of swords, it certainly
succeeded. But the social costs of these new features, and the questions
behind whether there is a better way, or if the number of swords even
matters, were never fully examined. Eventually, more price controls were
always introduced.

EL's initial success, and the guild's mirror of this growth, came from
the fact that it was actually fun to play. Despite the problems that players
had with the way the game was managed, they still kept coming back.
But, over time, EL lost old players faster than it picked up new ones.
There were updates that made the game look better, but they did not seem
to address the core concerns of the players, and a more complex system
made it more difficult for new players to understand how to play.

Google Trends shows that Eternal Lands peaked at 100 percent in
March 2006 and began a consistent decline after I quit the game for the
first time. Now it rarely sees more than 2 percent of this peak, and the

---

[1] It was only a few months later that I started deleting my data and erasing the history
of my time in Eternal Lands. This is the point where the preface begins.

game has nearly disappeared from history.[2] EL might never recapture the popularity that it once had, but I still consider it to be the best game that I've ever played. The flaws made it fun. The other players made it fun. Playing a part that I would never play in the real world also made it fun. But the best thing about EL was knowing that I could take what I discovered in the game and make it useful for understanding the real world.

By the end of my time in EL, pieces of RICH spawned five new guilds. Three former members become moderators. Two former members become developers for the game (with trollson and Lunksnark as development advisors). And I walked away with a story. The game still exists, and the guild still exists, but someday they will disappear. What remains will be the real-world ideas.

The Economics of Video Game Design (Incentives)

Former players uniformly consider Eternal Lands to be a mining simulator with a chat room attached or a chat room with a game on the side. However they described it, harvesting was by far the most prominent skill, and the game's culture was a big reason why so many players stuck around for so long. EL's design was not crisp, but it was actually a fun game, and the players who complained about it still played it. Part of the reason they stayed came from the fact that they had so many friends on the inside, and Entropy deserves credit for attracting these players in the first place.

In the Introduction, we described a good game as one with a basic skill system that progresses in a natural way and has an entertaining (or addictive) reward system. But it does take a little more than those two features, and the details behind EL's organization shows a few areas that can be improved. This is the economic perspective of the game creator.

Good games don't need amazing graphics—EL certainly did not have it—but they do need to give enough context to explain why the world is the way it is, and they need to offer players a way to feel like they're

---

[2] To be fair to Eternal Lands, the Google Trends search terms for MMORPG and Massively Multiplayer Online Role-Playing Game, and various other descriptions of similar online games, all peaked around August 2009 and followed EL's consistent decline.

becoming more powerful. EL's basic process followed the standard model for an online game:

1. Gather resources.
2. Transform the resources into metal bars.
3. Turn the metal bars into weapons and armor.
4. Use the weapons and armor (and other "side" skills such as magic, potions, and summoning) to support fighting skills.

It made sense, even if it was not immediately obvious. The skill system allowed EL players to build their characters however they wanted, and the difficulty scaled up with each level. The basic mechanics and structure were pretty good.

The social atmosphere was also attractive. Players were better off when they worked together, and the guild system gave them an efficient way of teaming up. Outlaws were easily identified, and there was usually open communication with the development team, so most players felt that they had a meaningful impact on the rest of the game. The game was also small enough that everyone could easily see how they were connected to everyone else, even if they saw each other as rivals. EL was effectively a social network with a game attached, but that made the game better.

All of these features are necessary for an attractive MMO, but they must be planned in a way that recognizes how each part relates to the rest of the game world. Because the EL world was built piece by piece without a full top-down review, the EL economic system was uneven. This is the part where, if I was designing my own video game economy, I would do things a little differently.

Every game world has a few useless items, but EL had entire categories of useless items. It had useless items that should be useful. The biggest example is the swords. The underlying factor behind what drives economics is incentives. The reason that there were so many unused swords is not because players enjoyed hoarding them, but because there were relatively strong incentives to produce the swords and very weak incentives for using the swords. The incentive for producers to level up was to mass-produce, increasing the supply and lowering the price. The incentive for consumers was to avoid using swords, lowering the demand and further lowering the price. If Entropy had changed the fighting system to encourage the use of swords, the demand would have been much stronger, and the excess that the sword market experienced would have never grown so large. There are two easy ways to do this: change the attack experience so that causing more damage would earn more experience (using swords would earn more attack experience); and add level requirements that prevent low-level players from using high-level products. These are extremely common game design choices that encourage players to use different weapons inside the game.

There was also a pricing problem throughout the entire economy. Part of this came from a few imbalances in the game's design, but another part was simply how the NPC prices were set. Most of their buy and sell prices were determined by a formula early in the game's history, before the consequences of those prices could be reviewed. The ideal solution is dynamic prices, where the NPC will lower their price each time a player sells and raise it each time a player buys (this is what RuneScape does). This would make a self-balancing system that is much closer to the real world.

Unfortunately, that type of system was beyond the reach of EL's development. But it was possible to manually adjust the NPC buy and sell prices. And whenever Entropy asked the players how he should fix the economy, the most popular suggestion was always changing NPC prices. But these were rarely adjusted. To be fair, fixing prices never works in the real world, and even minor adjustments could cause big changes that lead to more complaints (it's also useful to remember that you can't give the players everything they want—they will always say that they want things to be easy, but that's not what makes a good game). At a minimum, he could have set the NPC prices so that final goods had the same value as the sum of their parts, but it's a difficult position.

In Entropy's mind, there should not be any built-in advantage to producing one item over another, and there should not be any obvious advantage to using one item over another. Whenever a product became unprofitable, the producers should automatically switch to another item. He was mostly right. The best system would attempt to balance multiple factors:

- Prices
- Experience points
- The effort needed to produce the items
- How much benefit the players get from using the items

This balance needs to be maintained in a way that doesn't make the game too easy or too hard. If players are too powerful, they lose interest. If players can't figure out what to do, they switch to an easier game. This balance is nearly impossible to achieve on the first try. The easiest option is to let the game run for a while to see what builds up, and then make the adjustment. This is what Entropy did in the very beginning, when hyperinflation made it too easy to make money. After he reset the game, it became a different problem—too many swords instead of too much money. His solution for reducing the number of swords was complicated and exotic, but it fit the spirit of this idea.

The demand side also needs to be balanced. High-quality powerful items should only be available to high-level players. Low-level players should be limited to low-quality items. EL did not do this. It had a concentration of mostly the best products. With lower quality items, there was a large and growing amount of excess supply. To try to fix the problem of excess supply, Entropy began creating price controls by using NPCs to buy some supplies, changing the characteristics of worthless items, and creating new processes that used the products from an over-supplied market. The story provides our examples: When Entropy introduced new swords in the game, he attempted to design them with an exceptionally high cost, expecting it to automatically lead to a high value. But the market did not respond as he hoped. After the novelty of the new swords wore off, their demand deflated and the prices dropped. To stabilize their value, Entropy introduced an NPC that bought the swords and set a minimum price.

Another option was to change the game in ways that would change player preferences and create new demand for low-value products. The first item Entropy focused on was the steel two-edged sword. According to Entropy, there were too many of these swords in the game, and people were not using them fast enough, so he came up with a solution to increase the value of swords—use them for harvesting. When the idea was implemented, it achieved his goal of reducing the number of steel two-edged swords by creating a new demand. It was so successful that he used this idea on other swords as well. But this always created another pricing problem in the new markets, where Entropy was again forced to find new sources of demand.

This method of focusing on one item at a time, individually targeting each market, was too narrow, and it did not consider the second-order effects. By only looking at one market, Entropy ran the risk of disrupting other markets, where he would be forced to move his focus again and cause even more disruptions. He succeeded in preventing inflation, but the real solution he was looking for was broader than just trying to reduce the number of swords, or the number of essences, or whatever factor he happened to be looking at. Zooming out and looking at the big picture would have made his job much easier. But even then, it's nearly impossible to prevent players from exploiting any tiny advantage that they can find.

EL did have a few natural ways of taking items out of the game. Things could break, and an item could fail to be produced, but it didn't happen often. Since my time in EL, Entropy has added new skills, and the ability to make items that would disappear for double the experience. He also killed the lilac bush and neutralized the secret RICH mine. They're potentially steps in the right direction, but they're not comprehensive.

Whatever the solution, the overall theme is very simple: In game design, the economics are just as important as the technical aspects of writing computer code. To make a great game requires not only a playable console, but also an understanding of the incentives that drive the players' actions. When the markets are more complex, such as the ones in MMORPGs, economics is necessary to keep the game interesting.

If we translate this into the real world, it's the same theme. In government policy, the economics are just as important as the technical aspects of managing a government program. To make a meaningful impact requires not only a great idea, but also an understanding of the incentives that encourage desired behavior. All markets are complex, and economics is necessary to ensure that the incentives align with the goals.

But we have to understand it first.

APPENDIX A

Who Is Mr.Mind?

There are more people in the world who know me as Mr.Mind than by any other name. It's not completely unique, but it's a name that I came up with on my own. I first used it in a game called Diablo, a game where players play the part of a hero who fights demons. I chose to be a sorcerer, and I needed a name that fit the fighting style of a player who uses magic; one who chooses to use the mind over muscle. What I uncovered later, long after my story of Eternal Lands (EL) reached its conclusion, is that googling my own character's name, Mr.Mind, brings up several webpages about a DC comic book supervillain. That character was a two-inch worm with an extraordinary power—it could take over the minds of other villains and of regular people and control them. It used this power to create an evil army called the Monster Society of Evil, and it used that army to fight against the heroes. My version of becoming an infamous Mr.Mind, with my own evil organization (although not as evil as the comic book version), parallels this story. RICH was my Monster Society of Evil, and my form of mind control came from the power of experience points, a feature so enticing that it was capable of charming RICH enemies into helping a guild that they hated.

When I started playing Eternal Lands, I did not intend to play the part of a villain, and I was not seeking any kind of notoriety. My preferred place in EL history was somewhere in the background where no one would see me. But if I had stayed in that place, then I never would have had the freedom to experiment with a perspective that allows more creativity, because I would have been too concerned with how everyone else was playing the game. There is always a conflict between the way things have always been done and the possibility that there might be a better way. Becoming entrenched in one single way of looking at the world is an approach that *feels* like safety, but it's actually a trap that prevents any significant progress, and it creates the risk of getting stuck when the rest of the world moves on. It is a conflict and a legacy that played out when I shifted the game's culture from a focus on profitability to a focus on mass production. The ones who got left behind were the ones who refused to change their minds.

The economic way of thinking puts facts before feelings, but it's not callous or cruel; it is an objective evaluation that relies on evidence and enables new ideas to be considered. My experiments showed the best ways to make money in EL, and part of my conclusion was that destroying competitors helped RICH get richer. But the bigger picture, when it came to RICH members, was that *compassion* pays more than pressure. If no one was willing to work for me, then it would not matter how much time I put into my plans, because there would be no way to make them a reality. As the RICH leader, my responsibility was to make sure that RICH members continued to receive the best benefits in the game. It was not my concern whether the RICH outsiders agreed with my goals or resisted my influence on the market. When I made an evaluation based on the evidence of my experiments, I would use the methods that were supported by my data. If my way was better, then my way would win. If my way was not better, then I would find a different way. That process of trying new things was the fundamental difference between what I was doing and what everyone else was doing. My strategy was directed more by my customers and my workers than by my competitors, and it was supported by an economic way of thinking that was not afraid to fail.

The Memoir of Mr.Mind

My main goal in Eternal Lands was not to have the highest level, make the most friends, or even make the most money. My goal was just to be able to do anything that I wanted to do. And by the time I was ready to quit the game to go to college, I had achieved that goal. In the most basic definition of the term, I beat the game. But I did more than beat it: I permanently altered the entire structure and culture of Eternal Lands; I built the largest and most powerful guild in the game, which peaked at just over 200 members; and I made myself the richest and most famous player to ever play.

Before I left the game for the first time, I had to formally announce the guild's transition and remind my competitors why I was better than them. In the MMORPG acronym, sometimes people forget about the "role-play" part. The role I played as the founder of RICH, like an actor in a movie, was well-known—the self-promoting mastermind of EL's biggest business. However, unlike most movies, this time the bad guy actually won.

On April 27, 2006, just 13 months since I first took over as the guild master of RICH, I said goodbye to the game in a three-page forum post that detailed what I did and why I won. I started modestly with my title: *A New Age Dawns, The Memoir of Mr.Mind.*

> After over a year as the leader of RICH, I have decided that it is time for me to step down and allow a new leader's flag to be raised. But before I announce my successor, I have another thing to say. I am leaving this game.

> I am certain that this shocks many people, and many others will be throwing a party at the thought of me leaving, but it is absolutely undeniable that what I have done in this game cannot be duplicated. (Mr.Mind 2006)

I described my goals in the game as a single-minded quest to ruin the entire economy and take down my market rivals. I played into the reputation that I encouraged for my character. I even went as far as calling Ember's murder "one of the most satisfying things I've ever done," while explaining away Richery's ban as being "reminded of the rules." I outlined the methods that I used to take over the market, including the way I "sold" experience points to new players in exchange for their labor. I detailed every major decision that led to making RICH the most powerful market force in Eternal Lands, moving from dominating the manufacturing market, to exploiting the alchemy market, and finally imploding the crafting market. I explained how I built the game's largest army of workers, and how I used their labor as a weapon in the war against the market. I reveled in the description of how my low prices killed my competitors' businesses. I was the best, I built the best and biggest guild, and I created an empire that would last for a long time after I left. RICH won. RICH would *always* win. I ended my post with a proud review of my character's goals:

> Having heard all of the nasty things that other suppliers have said about me, I begin to feel contented that even if my vision [of total market destruction] did not become a reality, I have ruined enough people to be satisfied with the results. After realizing this, along with the fact that there is nothing in the game that I can't make, I decided that it is time for me to move on.

> My leaving may bring up the question of where RICH's new leadership will guide the guild. So with the future in mind, I have left RICH to its most loyal supporting member, Richery. A few things will change, but RICH will definitely never be poor, and the brilliant minds I have worked with will never fail to out-think everyone else. (Mr.Mind 2006)

The topic was almost immediately locked. The moderators, unable to keep up with monitoring the post, were forced to close it every few hours just to hold back the intensity of the responses. My way of playing the game was controversial, and the way that players outside of RICH responded to my market influence (and my gloating about my market influence) reflected that controversy. No one disputed these accomplishments, but they were undecided on whether I was good for the game. The conversation that followed my retirement speech was a heated debate over the morals of my methods and the purpose of my experiment. It varied between complete rage and casual admiration.

Thoughts from RICH Outsiders

The players questioned how I should be viewed. Was Mr.Mind just a pioneering entrepreneur who chased an opportunity that nobody else could see? Or was Mr.Mind a shameless capitalist who made a guild of slave workers and broke rules to cheat for an advantage? (Did Mr.Mind have mind control powers that fooled these players into working for him?)

And why try to break a game that's made to be fun? I stayed silent as I watched the responses roll in. The angry players got there first.

> I'm glad you're leaving because you screwed the market.. But you're actually proud you did it? (OMG, you're such a bastard). ... I think the community would've been better off if you just destroyed the guild. You guys did nothing bad to the community by screwing the market. Yes, I will have a party because you're leaving. (Gohan 2006)

> I find your attitude and social conscience appalling. It's exactly this sort of self-serving, ego boosting and 'one fingered salute' attitude I rail against every day. (Chance 2006)

> He's long said that he's pointing out the problems in the economy so that they get fixed ... right, so do it once, prove it, and then leave it alone till it's fixed. That's the right thing to do. (ttlanhil 2006)

> Damn, you are so ... full of yourself. (Nidan 2006)

> If breaking something is a goal in itself ... well, I think it's a sad and not that honourable one. But this topic doesn't really bring anything new: we all knew rich's goals for ages, we all knew that most of its leaders team was ... self-satisfied. (Cayuga 2006)

One player was more upset than the others. Her tirade, which ran several pages, contained the most elegant online insult that I have ever seen.

> He is nothing more than an egotistical arrogant worthless piece of digital shrapnel floating around in the cyberspace environment. ... He simply played a game and his game was to get rich and piss people off. He succeeded in that but that's it. Nothing more. If I'm not mistaken he was banned a few times and so was his bot for multiplay and he was made pkable also several times for breaking this rule or that rule. That was probably all part of his game too ... oh yeah, bravo MrMind!! (Enyo 2006).

When other players accused her of having an unfairly harsh opinion, she doubled down in another post.

The reasons that he isn't enamored have nothing to do with the economy but rather his total disrespect for others: players, the mod/devs, the rules and the game in general. ... His attitude was and still is appalling. ... The only reason he chose NOW to post his "goodbye" post is because now is when this huge economical debate is going on, thus putting the spotlight on him and his need for attention and recognition ... even negative recognition is good for him because it's still attention and he is feeding off of that. Bravo bravo bravoooooooooooo MrMind! (Enyo 2006).

They all had more to say, and there were others who wanted to say their piece, but the moderators were cutting off anyone who responded with too much rage. I found it unfortunate, because exploring the raw emotions behind my market actions was a major part of the informal experiment. I had accepted the reputation that RICH was given when Ember labeled the guild as a group of outlaws, and I transformed it into an asset for the guild that enabled RICH to focus on market manipulation. I was famously consistent with my words and my methods. Everyone knew my views on the market, and everyone knew that I would follow through on what I said I would do, even if the things I said were unpopular. My commitment to the character was even admired by one of the moderators. He compared me to the players who complained about my attitude by questioning their need for attention. He said, "Unlike you he is refreshingly open about his gargantuan ego." (the_antiroot 2006).

On the other hand, the other players in the game had some good reasons to be angry. I contributed to the slaughter of an innocent player. I provoked attention by breaking rules in front of moderators (and I kept getting away with it). I got rich by wrecking an entire economic system. And the worst part, the part that made people hate me the most, was that I didn't even pretend to feel bad about it. Instead, I celebrated my guild's achievements.

It was still the market competition that made people rage the most, because this was the part where RICH directly affected everyone else. The confusing question here is why they got angry before objectively examining my methods. Why didn't they all just start doing what I was doing? Why resist the RICH disruptions? The easy answer is that it's hard for people to admit when they're wrong, and nobody likes to lose control of their space in the market. But that would not tell the whole story. It was genuinely unfair for people with real jobs to have to compete with a high-school kid on summer break who treated the game like a full-time job, and the RICH way of playing was admittedly sucking the fun out of the game. It was also impossible for a smaller guild to keep up with the kind of production that RICH was outputting, even if they wanted to use the same strategy. I was also taking credit for something that was not entirely under my control. Because leveling up in the game required mass production, the market prices would have continued falling even without the influence of RICH. My contributions only served to accelerate the game's ever-increasing supply and force prices to move lower at a faster pace. But since the rest of the game had always accused me of causing the market's problems, I was gladly willing to accept that infamy, because more infamy ironically meant more business; having a well-known reputation for keeping the cheapest prices brought the customers to RICH and Richery.[1]

The next group of responses was more accepting. Entropy started off the casual admirers:

Personally, I find this post to be very informative, and I don't understand why you guys decry his actions. It's [just a] game after all, and not only that, but he didn't macro or anything, he had access to the same methods you did ... Kudos to him. (Entropy 2006)

And more came in.

Personally, I never liked the tactics—whether or not I would have figured out the tactic myself is immaterial, as I personally couldn't do it

---

[1] I privately messaged some of the critics to tell them that my attitude was just part of the game and explained that what I said about my character was actually me playing a character. I also confessed that I knew the market would have changed even without my influence on the game. They all accepted my reasoning and eventually came to admire my honesty, but I let the public record stand.

myself. He did it, he grew in wealth, and he had the shattered dreams of some other players on him—still, I felt it best to remain civil. I hated the tactics, but I could never hate the person. (Arnieman 2006)

I think what he did was certainly impressive ... but I liken it to big business vs small business. If you get the resources together then you can undercut and wipe out all competitors. Most people don't like this sort of approach [in real life], and likewise, in-game. I agree, kudos to him for achieving what he did ... however, this is a game and it is meant to be fun for all of us. (Torg 2006)

Even a moderator offered high praise, separating what I did from how I did it: "I have no interest in whether folks class his actions as right or wrong ... I personally feel that only a fool would not recognise him as the foremost authority on EL's economy." (the_antiroot 2006).

Some players were simply amazed by the time it took to build RICH: "Oh ...... well it is a game, with reasonable freedom to be played as you see fit. But did Mr.Mind really spend a percentage of his free time just doing that??? WOW" (vampireLOREN 2006).

Another friendly player suggested that my story could fit in with other famous cases in business history, comparing me with John Rockefeller, "who formed the company Standard Oil by expanding both vertically (such as the drilling, transportation, selling, and storage for oil) and horizontally (forcing competitors to go out of business and buying them up at cheap prices)." Then they pivoted, suggesting that

Mr. Mind can also be compared to Jeffrey Skilling, in a way, former CFO of ENRON if anyone remembers that particular scandal. ENRON's tactics to exploit the new deregulation policies in California strikes a remarkable parallel to the way Mr. Mind has exploited the manufacturing and alchemy economy. (Kendai 2006)

The description was fair, and it ended with an apology. "Mr. Mind, I'm sorry if these comparisons seem unfair to you, although knowing you, I think you would rather enjoy them." I was entertained (Kendai 2006).

The truth is that the last comparisons may have been the most appropriate. I did have some dark secrets. If anyone knew that I had betrayed my own brother to take control of RICH, then they might have been a little less forgiving, but the secret RICH mine—created by a former RICH member just for the benefit of RICH (when they promised to put the game's interests above the guild's)—crossed the line from capitalism to corruption. RICH had an influence on the game's design that was a little *too* powerful. Other players eventually found the mine, and most high-level players shared in the benefits from using it, but I can't imagine the response from anyone who might have learned that it was made for RICH.

Thoughts from RICH Insiders

I did not ask Eon_Schmidt to do any favors for RICH, but when he told me about his plans to create a secret RICH mine, I didn't say no, either. He agreed to the same rules as everyone else who joined the development and moderation teams. Anyone in RICH had to leave RICH to be considered for those positions, and everyone had to promise not to help RICH in any way. And even after making that commitment, he still chose to remain loyal. What's remarkable is that Eon_Schmidt's loyalty to RICH was not unusual. Outsiders often described the guild as a group of slaves who were fooled into making Mr.Mind rich (the two-inch worm's mind control powers seem to be a fitting comparison). But that's not quite true. *Everyone* in RICH became rich. Everyone was well-paid, even if most of their pay came in the form of experience points. But you still can't buy the kind of loyalty that comes from someone like Eon_Schmidt. The responses from former RICH members made this clear.

> Everyone in the guild was quite friendly. I did not meet any bloodsucking, economy ruining Walmart executives. MrMind did a very good job of *convincing* members and non-members to produce items. ... And noobs benefited along with the guild. "The

economy needs to be fixed" was the rallying cry on the forums. Who was upset? Not the noobs, but rather the people who previously held control of the economy. ... But, come on people, this is a GAME! "social conscience"... HA! The economy is fake! ... Some of you need a taste of reality. (Octane 2006)

The man has a legacy in EL that will be passed down for some time. ... So he under-cut some in game prices? Entropy put it well ... it's [just a] game. (Evalin 2006)

Another former member added his own perspective.

I didn't know it then, but the view from inside was much more different than what others would think. It is clear that many people here hate him for ruining a ~~real~~ EL Market (hey...it's only a game, right?), but I disagree. If the factors were the same as they were back then, then the market "would have declined anyway" and one can only hasten this irreversible process, adapt and exploit the lucrative market. (MagpieLee 2006)

It was SiKiK, the only current RICH member to respond, who gave the best explanation of what it meant to be RICH.

Personally I find the idea that MM has exploited some of us quite interesting, particularly as I, for one, have never felt that way (or maybe this is one of MM's skills—making us feel like we haven't been exploited, when in fact we have all been "done over"?). ... Put it like this - I joined RICH as a newb during the "100k FE" project and have been with them ever since. The free ingredients and [experience points] were great as a newb (would have taken me ages to harvest all that stuff myself), and I was happy to give away my FE's, bars, etc. in the knowledge that I would always have access to high end goods (weapons, armour etc. for free). ... I doubt i would have made it to level 50 crafting so quickly if I had not had the assistance of a helpful, intelligent and enterprising guild. If I have been a "paid employee" for MM over the last 12 months, then I can highly recommend the remuneration package—a smeg load of [experience points], massive amounts of [gold coins] and all the [serpent swords] you can eat. (SiKiK 2006)

The people from inside RICH all insisted that I was good at *convincing* everyone to help me. They said that I paid the best, and that the market wars were just part of the game (one old member later suggested that I should be called "Mr. Kind" for my generosity and attention).[2] The people on the outside either praised my command of the game's economy or raged at my lack of empathy. There was one outsider, however, who could see from the RICH insider's perspective. Someone on the outside could finally explain how I did what I did.

He gave his post a clever title. "Do poachers make the best gamekeepers? Ideas from Mr. Mind." He restated the methods that I described. "It's a simple business plan. Effectively selling experience to newbies, but getting around the obvious fact that most newbs have little gold by getting them to pay in labour." (Mundaus 2006). He acknowledged the praise that I received from the other players.

He deserves respect for noticing and exploiting the high implicit [gold coin] price applied to [experience points]. Anyone can still do this, just post in market channel "Mixer wanted for 5k FEs" or somesuch and there'll be no shortage of volunteers. … This is perfectly sensible from the point of view of the mixers as well - for new players, [experience points] have an especially high value. (Mundaus 2006)

Then he summarized the secret that launched me to the top of Eternal Lands.

The lesson we should learn from Mr. Mind's success is this: [experience points] have a very high implicit [gold coin] price, especially to new players. The best way to get [experience points] is mass production. Thus there is a very strong pressure applied

---

[2]Personal communication with Jaynix (March 1, 2016).

that means players (i) Make lots of items (ii) Are happy to sell at
a price that gives a [gold coin] loss, but an (implicit) profit when
the value of [experience points] is factored in. (Mundaus 2006)

Now everyone knew what I had been doing all along.

In the end, it was a polarizing discussion, one so passionate that the
moderators were forced to continue locking and unlocking the topic just
to catch up with the complaints. After two days, they gave up and closed
it for good. Whether the players liked me or hated me, they all recognized
that I would leave as one of the Eternal Lands' legends, and no one would
ever be able to repeat the rise of another RICH.

APPENDIX B

Concepts by Chapter

This appendix is an outline of which topics each chapter emphasizes. It is broken down into four separate categories:

- New topics that are introduced in the book for the first time
- Topics revisited that are re-introduced or reinforced after already being defined in an earlier chapter
- Real-world examples that show the connection from the game world to the real world
- General discussion topics that are not explicitly mentioned in the chapter but form the basis for questions that can further explore important economic, business, and ethical ideas

For all of these categories, there is a mix of basic definitions, individual decisions, firm decisions, and regulator/creator decisions.

Topics for Discussion

- **Introduction**
  - New Topics: Functions of Money; Hyperinflation
  - Real-World Examples: Weimar Republic
  - General Discussion: Entertainment in Economics; The Evolution of Video Games
- **Part I: The Market**
  - Chapter 1: Hunting Rabbits, Picking Flowers
    - New Topics: Opportunity Cost; Barriers to Entry; Scarcity; Price Floor; Price Ceiling; Raw Materials; Intermediate Goods; Finished Products

- Real-World Examples: Industries with Barriers to Entry; Prominent Industries and Products for Each Type of Good
- General Discussion: Market Structure; Types of Goods; Price Controls
  - Chapter 2: RIVA
    - New Topics: Supply; Demand; Market Equilibrium; Inputs and Outputs; Land, Labor, Capital, and Entrepreneurship; Economies of Scale; Reputational Capital
    - Real-World Examples: Henry Ford's assembly line; Chipotle's *e coli* scare
    - General Discussion: The Interaction of Inputs and Outputs; Efficiency and Specialization; The Value of Reputation
- **Part II: A New Guild**
  - Chapter 3: RICH Is Born
    - New Topics: The Law of Demand; Perfectly Competitive Markets
    - Real-World Examples: Grain
    - General Discussion: Learning by Doing; Price Takers
  - Chapter 4: The Dying Ember
    - New Topics: Boycotts
    - Topics Revisited: Reputational Capital
    - Real-World Examples: Chick-fil-A; Monsanto
    - General Discussion: Ethical Concerns for an Outlaw; Ethical Concerns of a Hostile Takeover
  - Chapter 5: Join Guild RICH
    - New Topics: Monopolistic Competition; Constraints; Cost-Benefit Analysis; Explicit Costs; Implicit Costs; Human Capital; Positive Externalities; Negative Externalities
    - Topics Revisited: Perfectly Competitive Market; Opportunity Cost; Land, Labor, Capital, and Entrepreneurship
    - Real-World Examples: Restaurants
    - General Discussion: Motivation from a Huge Goal; Escaping Direct Competition; Incentives and Rewards; The Value of Time; Trading Labor for Experience and Human Capital; Externalities

- **Part III: The Rise of RICH**
  - ○ Chapter 6: Market War I
    - New Topics: The Law of Supply; Cartel
    - Topics Revisited: Supply; Perfectly Competitive Markets
    - Real-World Examples: OPEC
    - General Discussion: Price Manipulation; A Failed Cartel; Importance of Understanding Market Structure
  - ○ Chapter 7: The Guild Party
    - New Topics: Vertical Integration
    - Topics Revisited: Specialization; Economies of Scale; Human Capital; Raw Materials; Intermediate Goods; Finished Goods
    - Real-World Examples: Carnegie Steel Company; Apple
    - General Discussion: Advantages of Competent Leadership Team; Organizational Structure; Advantages of Efficiency and Scale
  - ○ Chapter 8: The Wal-Mart of Eternal Lands
    - New Topics: Inferior Goods; Normal Goods; Substitute Goods; Complement Goods; Substitution Effect; Income Effect; Arbitrage
    - Topics Revisited: Supply and Demand; Perfectly Competitive Markets; Price Floor; Vertical Integration; Human Capital; Predatory Pricing
    - Real-World Examples: Spam; Wal-Mart; Standard Oil; Carnegie Steel
    - General Discussion: Price Interaction between Goods; Effectiveness of Price Floors; Concerns about Predatory Pricing
  - ○ Chapter 9: The Crafting Market Collapse
    - New Topics: Consumable Goods; Durable Goods; Demand Shift; Supply Shift; Elasticity; Cross-Price Elasticity of Demand; Monopoly; Natural Monopoly; Horizontal Integration
    - Topics Revisited: Intermediate Goods; Vertical Integration; Supply and Demand; Substitute Goods; Predatory Pricing; Barriers to Entry

- - Real-World Examples: Examples of Natural Monopolies; Disney's Horizontal Integration
  - General Discussion: Using Real Money to Buy Items inside the Game; Premium Pricing; Fair Payments and Working For "Free"; Prices Collapsing to Zero
  - ○ Chapter 10: The RICH Effect
    - New Topics: Regulatory Barrier to Entry
    - Topics Revisited: Supply Shift; Arbitrage
    - Real-World Examples: Utilities and Licenses
    - General Discussion: Low-Cost Providers and Deflation; Market Power and Political Conflict; Government-Protected Competitive Positions
  - ○ Chapter 11: Market War II
    - Topics Revisited: Economies of Scale; Monopoly; Cartel; Boycott; Opportunity Cost
    - Real-World Examples: Wal-Mart
    - General Discussion: Merits of a Market Strike; Economic Unfairness; Reputation as Advertising; Competitive Advantages; Failed Boycotting; Market Changes
  - ○ Chapter 12: Market War III
    - New Topics: Price Dumping; Market Corner; Economic Profits
    - Topics Revisited: Anti-Competitive Behavior; Predatory Pricing; Natural Monopoly; Cartel; Supply; Demand; Arbitrage; Implicit Costs; Explicit Costs
    - Real-World Examples: Microsoft; Google; Hunt Brothers
    - General Discussion: Predatory Pricing; Market Wars; Time and Money; Incentives
- **Part IV: The Game Changes**
  - ○ Chapter 13: Cooldown
    - Topics Revisited: Incentives; Cost-Benefit Analysis; Opportunity Cost
    - Real-World Examples: Extreme Couponers
    - General Discussion: Time and Money; Scale; Unintended Consequences of New Regulation

Glossary

arbitrage. Buying a product or resource in one market and selling it in a different market to take advantage of a price difference.

barriers to entry. A feature that makes it difficult to enter a new market, such as startup costs or government regulations.

boycotts. Avoiding a specific producer's products or services. The purpose of a boycott is to encourage an organization or a person to change their behavior.

capital. The equipment used for production.

cartel. A group of suppliers that agree to fix prices.

complement goods. Goods that are generally bought at the same time and are used together.

constraints. Limitations based on scarcity.

consumable goods. Products that can only be used once.

cost-benefit analysis. A comparison between costs and benefits.

cross-price elasticity of demand. How much the demand for a product changes when the price of another product changes.

demand. The amount that consumers are willing and able to buy at each price.

durable goods. Products that last for a long time.

economic profits. A measure of profit that includes the opportunity cost of alternative investments.

economies of scale. When increasing the size of the production operation leads to lower costs.

elasticity. Elasticity measures how much the sales of a product respond to a change in price. The more responsive the product is to a change in price, the more elastic it is.

entrepreneurship. The leadership that makes production plans and strategic business or market plans.

experience points. Every action related to a skill earns experience points for that specific skill. Earning enough experience points allows a player to advance to the next level.

explicit costs. Costs that are paid.

finished products. The end result of the manufacturing process. The final products that are sold to consumers.

forum. An online forum is a message board devoted to a specific topic. In the context of Eternal Lands, the official EL forum is the place where EL players discuss issues related to the game. Some groups within the game also have their own forum.

guild. A formal group of players in Eternal Lands that choose to associate with each other.

guild master. A guild leader in Eternal Lands.

horizontal integration. An attempt to concentrate market power at the same stage of production.

human capital. The quality of a person's skills, experience, and knowledge. A highly skilled, experienced, and knowledgeable worker is more valuable than an average worker.

hyperinflation. An extreme case of inflation where the amount of money introduced into the economic system accelerates while prices are rising out of control.

implicit costs. Hidden costs that are not directly paid.

income effect. Consumers become indirectly wealthier when prices fall.

inferior goods. Generally lower-quality goods. Consumers will buy more inferior goods when their income goes down, and buy fewer when their income goes up.

inputs. Resources that are used to make other products.

intermediate goods. The processed raw materials that have been upgraded into something more useful for the next step of manufacturing.

labor. The people who work for the producer.

land. The land used for production.

law of demand. Consumers will be willing and able to buy more of a product as the price goes down.

law of supply. Producers will be willing and able to sell more of their product as the price goes up.

market corner. An attempt to control a market by purchasing all of the supply in the market.

market equilibrium. The quantity and price where demand matches supply.

moderator. A player who volunteers to enforce the games rules. A moderator is granted special powers by the game creator.

monopolistic competition. A market with a large number of competitors offering similar products that can be differentiated.

monopoly. A market where one firm is the only supplier in the market.

natural monopoly. A market where one company can produce its products at a lower cost than any other potential competitor.

negative externalities. A situation where the costs from one market are paid somewhere else. It leads to too much investment in markets that have side-effects such as pollution.

non-player character (npc). An NPC is an automated character controlled by the programming inside a game, rather than a player. It does whatever function the game creator commands it to do.

normal goods. A good that consumers will buy more of when their income goes up.

oligopoly. A market with a small number of large, powerful producers.

opportunity cost. The cost of giving up the next best alternative.

outputs. The products that come out of a production process.

perfectly competitive market. A market with a large number of buyers and sellers who all sell exactly the same product, and none of them are big enough to influence the price in any meaningful way.

player killing (pk). Player killing, known as "pk," is simply the act of killing another player (instead of killing a monster). Only specifically marked areas allow pk.

positive externalities. A situation where an investment in one area leads to benefits somewhere else. Since the organization making the investment does not directly see all of the benefits, they do not invest as much as they should. This leads to underinvestment in areas that produce positive externalities, such as education, health care, and infrastructure.

price ceiling. An artificial limit to how high a market price can go. It is only effective if the normal market price is higher than the price ceiling.

price dumping. When a company sells its products for a loss to force competitors out of business.

price floor. An artificial limit to how low a market price can go. It is only effective if the normal market price is lower than the price floor.

principal/agent problem. When there is someone who makes decisions on behalf of other people, but also has powerful incentives to put their own interests first.

raw materials. The basic unprocessed materials that are used to make other goods.

regulatory barrier to entry. A barrier to entry that is created and supported by government regulations.

regulatory capture. When an organization created to keep a market fair is infected by the firms that it's meant to regulate, and it ends up advancing those firms' interests over the society's interests.

reputational capital. The value and goodwill that comes from being known as an ethical or trustworthy organization or person. It takes a long time to build and only minutes to destroy, and it can go negative.

scarcity. The economic description of how we make decisions based on a limited amount of resources and theoretically unlimited demands.

second-order effects. When one change leads to primary change, and that primary change leads to another, secondary change.

substitute goods. When two similar goods serve the same function and one can be swapped out for the other.

substitution effect. Lowering the price for one good reduces the demand for a substitute good.

sunk cost. A cost that has already been spent, cannot be recovered, and should not be considered.

supply. The amount that producers are willing and able to sell at each price.

vertical integration. A vertically integrated organization is one that does each step of the production process all on its own. They follow the entire production process, from gathering raw materials, to transforming them into intermediate goods, to making and selling the finished goods at the end.

Bibliography

Aislinn. February 19, 2009. "RE: Is My Character Locked? [Online forum comment]." http://www.eternal-lands.com/forum/index.php?/topic/48489-is-my-character-locked/&do=findComment&comment=488507,(accessed June 29, 2018).

Aislinn. July 24, 2005. "RE: Richery [Online forum comment]." http://www.eternal-lands.com/forum/index.php?/topic/16625-richery/&do=findComment&comment=182653, (accessed October 25, 2016).

Aislinn. July 25, 2005. "RE: Richery [Online forum comment]." http://www.eternal-lands.com/forum/index.php?/topic/16625-richery/&do=findComment&comment=182860, (accessed October 25, 2016).

Aislinn. July 24, 2005. "RE: Richery [Online forum comment]." http://www.eternal-lands.com/forum/index.php?/topic/16625-richery/&do=findComment&comment=182717, (accessed October 25, 2016).

Ariely, D. 2009. *Predictably Irrational: The Hidden Forces That Shape Our Decisions.* New York, NY: HarperCollins.

Arnieman. April 27, 2006. "RE: A New Age Dawns, The Memoir of Mr.Mind [Online forum comment]." http://www.eternal-lands.com/forum/index.php?/topic/24738-a-new-age-dawns/&do=findComment&comment=261257, (accessed June 3, 2008).

Arnieman. September 28, 2005. "RE: Crafter's Strike, Crafter's Strike and Why You Should Join [Online forum comment]." http://www.eternal-lands.com/forum/index.php?/topic/18519-crafters-strike/&do=findComment&comment=202521, (accessed November 29, 2008).

Arnieman. October 1, 2005. "RE: RICH Services [Online forum comment]." http://www.eternal-lands.com/forum/index.php?/topic/16560-rich-services/&do=findComment&comment=203699, (accessed March 29, 2018).

Arnieman. October 1, 2005. "RE: RICH Services [Online forum comment]." http://www.eternal-lands.com/forum/index.php?/topic/16560-rich-services/&do=findComment&comment=203864, (accessed March 29, 2018).

Bajarin, B. July 1, 2011. "Why Competing with Apple Is So Difficult." http://techland.time.com/2011/07/01/why-competing-with-apple-is-so-difficult/, (accessed August 21, 2018).

Beattie, A. February 16, 2018. "AT&T: One of the Successful Spinoffs in History." https://www.investopedia.com/ask/answers/09/att-breakup-spinoff.asp, (accessed June 28, 2018).

behindthemask08. December 25, 2004. "Selling Everything I Have [Online forum comment]." http://www.eternal-lands.com/forum/index.php?/topic/10763-selling-everything-i-have/, (accessed June 27, 2018).

bkc56. April 24, 2006. "RE: Fixing Some of the Economy [Online forum comment]." http://www.eternal-lands.com/forum/index.php?/topic/24624-fixing-some-of-the-economy/&page=2&tab=comments#comment-260376, (accessed November 29, 2008).

Brodwin, E. June 7, 2018. "After a $66 billion merger, one of the most hated food companies in the world is disappearing - sort of." https://www.businessinsider.com/monsanto-beyer-merge-drop-monsanto-name-2018-6, (accessed August 21, 2018).

Cain, A. September 26, 2018. "The Rise and Fall of the Company Behind 'Reader Rabbit' and all Your Favorite Educational Games." https://theoutline.com/post/6293/reader-rabbit-history-the-learning-company-zoombinis-carmen-sandiego?zd=2&zi=xyhfl3jw, (accessed December 6, 2018).

Castronova, E. 2005. *Synthetic Worlds: The Business and Culture of Online Games*. Chicago, IL: The University of Chicago Press.

Cayuga. April 28, 2006. "RE: A New Age Dawns, The Memoir of Mr.Mind [Online forum comment]." http://www.eternal-lands.com/forum/index.php?/topic/24738-a-new-age-dawns/&do=findComment&comment=261332, (accessed June 3, 2008).

Chance. April 27, 2006. "RE: A New Age Dawns, The Memoir of Mr.Mind [Online forum comment]." http://www.eternal-lands.com/forum/index.php?/topic/24738-a-new-age-dawns/&do=findComment&comment=261233, (accessed June 3, 2008).

Chernow, R. 1998. *Titan: The Life of John D. Rockefeller, Sr.* New York, NY: Vintage Books.

Christopher, B. August 16, 2016. "How the Hunt Brothers Cornered the Silver Market and Then Lost It All." https://priceonomics.com/how-the-hunt-brothers-cornered-the-silver-market/, (accessed March 29, 2018).

Collins, J., and J.I. Porras. 2002. *Built to Last: Successful Habits of Visionary Companies*. New York, NY: HarperBusiness.

Colossus. November 27, 2003. "Prices on Web Site verses Game [Online forum comment]." http://www.eternal-lands.com/forum/index.php?/topic/164-prices-on-web-site-verses-game/, (accessed April 19, 2018).

Conroy, M. 2004. *500 Comic Book Villains*. Hauppauge, NY: Barrons.

Crunchbase Inc. 2018. "The Walt Disney Company > Acquisitions." https://www.crunchbase.com/organization/the-walt-disney-company/acquisitions/acquisitions_list#section-acquisitions, (accessed March 26, 2018).

Danforth, W.H. 2002. *I Dare You!* St. Louis, MO: American Youth Foundation.

Daxon. March 28, 2005. "RE: hEaL Mebers and Allies [Online forum comment]." http://www.eternal-lands.com/forum/index.php?/topic/13431-heal-mebers-and-allies/&do=findComment&comment=147903, (accessed July 20, 2010).

Desjardins, J. November 24, 2017. "Chart: The Evolution of Standard Oil." http://www.visualcapitalist.com/chart-evolution-standard-oil/, (accessed June 23, 2018).

Dibbell, J. 2006. *Play Money: Or, How I Quit My Day Job and Made Millions Trading Virtual Loot*. New York, NY: Basic Books.

Dorsey, P. 2004. *The Five Rules for Successful Stock Investing: Morningstar's Guide to Building Wealth and Winning in the Market*. Hoboken, NJ: John Wiley & Sons.

Dorsey, P. 2008. *The Little Book That Builds Wealth: The Knockout Formula for Finding Great Investments*. Hoboken, NJ: John Wiley & Sons.

DrMabuse. September 28, 2005. "Crafter's Strike, Crafter's Strike and Why You Should Join [Online forum comment]." http://www.eternal-lands.com/forum/index.php?/topic/18519-crafters-strike/, (accessed November 29, 2008).

DrMabuse. September 29, 2005. "RE: Crafter's Strike, Crafter's Strike and Why You Should Join [Online forum comment]." http://www.eternal-lands.com/forum/index.php?/topic/18519-crafters-strike/&do=findComment&comment=202795, (accessed November 29, 2008).

Dubner, S.J. January 21, 2016. Do Boycotts Work? http://freakonomics.com/podcast/do-boycotts-work-a-new-freakonomics-radio-podcast/, (accessed August 21, 2018).

Economist. December 23, 1999. "Standard ogre—Millennium issue: Antitrust." https://www.economist.com/business/1999/12/23/standard-ogre, (accessed March 29, 2018).

Ember. March 28, 2005. "hEaL Mebers and Allies [Online forum comment]." http://www.eternal-lands.com/forum/index.php?/topic/13431-heal-mebers-and-allies/, (accessed July 20, 2010).

Entropy. December 8, 2005. "Cooldown Log [Online forum comment]." http://www.eternal-lands.com/forum/index.php?/topic/20845-cooldown-log/, (accessed June 23, 2018).

Entropy. January 31, 2006. "Guild Owned NPCs (Merchants) [Online forum comment]." http://www.eternal-lands.com/forum/index.php?/topic/22273-guild-owned-npcs-merchants/, (accessed June 28, 2018).

Entropy. November 20, 2003. "News from the Old Site [Online forum comment]." http://www.eternal-lands.com/forum/index.php?/topic/12-news-from-the-old-site/, (accessed August 11, 2018).

Entropy. April 27, 2006. "RE: A New Age Dawns, The Memoir of Mr.Mind [Onlineforumcomment]."http://www.eternal-lands.com/forum/index.php?/topic/24738-a-new-age-dawns/&do=findComment&comment=261248, (accessed June 3, 2008).

Entropy. July 25, 2005. "RE: Richery [Online forum comment]." http://www.eternal-lands.com/forum/index.php?/topic/16625-richery/&do=findComment&comment=182884, (accessed October 25, 2016).

Enyo. April 28, 2006. "RE: A New Age Dawns, The Memoir of Mr.Mind [Online forum comment]." http://www.eternal-lands.com/forum/index.php?/topic/24738-a-new-age-dawns/&do=findComment&comment=261456, (accessed June 3, 2008).

Enyo. April 29, 2006. "RE: A New Age Dawns, The Memoir of Mr.Mind [Online forum comment]." http://www.eternal-lands.com/forum/index.php?/topic/24738-a-new-age-dawns/&do=findComment&comment=261577, (accessed June 3, 2008).

Evalin. April 28, 2006. "RE: A New Age Dawns, The Memoir of Mr.Mind [Online forum comment]." http://www.eternal-lands.com/forum/index.php?/topic/24738-a-new-age-dawns/&do=findComment&comment=261494, (accessed June 3, 2008).

Fergusson, A. 2010. *When Money Dies: The Nightmare of Deficit Spending, Devaluation, and Hyperinflation in Weimar Germany.* New York, NY: PublicAffairs.

Fishman, C. 2007. *The Wal-Mart Effect.* 2nd. London, England: Penguin Books.

Fitzpatrick, A. November 5, 2014. "A Judge Ordered Microsoft to Split. Here's Why It's Still a Single Company." http://time.com/3553242/microsoft-monopoly/, (accessed March 29, 2018).

flinto. January 29, 2006. "Production Cost Calculations [Online forum comment]." http:// www.eternal-lands.com/forum/index.php?/topic/22190-production-cost-calculations/, (accessed November 29, 2009).

gadai. September 29, 2005. "RE: Crafter's Strike, Crafter's Strike and Why You Should Join [Online forum comment]." http://www.eternal-lands.com/forum/index.php?/topic/18519-crafters-strike/&do=findComment&comment=202942, (accessed November 29, 2008).

gadai. September 30, 2005. "RE: RICH Services [Online forum comment]." http://www.eternal-lands.com/forum/index.php?/topic/16560-rich-services/&do=findComment&comment=203067, (accessed March 29, 2018).

gadai. September 30, 2005. "RE: RICH Services [Online forum comment]." http://www.eternal-lands.com/forum/index.php?/topic/16560-rich-services/&do=findComment&comment=203085, (accessed March 29, 2018).

Galbraith, J.K. 1997. *The Great Crash 1929*. New York, NY: Houghton Mifflin Company.

Gee, J.P. 2007. *What Video Games Have to Teach Us About Learning And Literacy*. New York, NY: Palgrave Macmillan.

Ghrae. 2005. "Fire Essence Details." http://www.el-cel.com/info/items_detail.php?Det=54, (accessed June 3, 2008).

Ghrae. 2005. "Iron Bar Details." http://www.el-cel.com/info/items_detail.php?Det=65, (accessed June 3, 2008).

Ghrae. September 25, 2005. "RE: Crafter's Strike, Crafter's Strike and Why You Should Join [Online forum comment]." http://www.eternal-lands.com/forum/index.php?/topic/18519-crafters-strike/&do=findComment&comment=202704, (accessed November 29, 2008).

Ghrae. July 24, 2005. "RE: Richery [Online forum comment]." http://www.eternal-lands.com/forum/index.php?/topic/16625-richery/&do=findComment&comment=182726, (accessed October 25, 2016).

Ghrae. 2005. "Steel Bar Details."   http://www.el-cel.com/info/items_detail.php?Det=66, (accessed June 3, 2008).

Ghrae. 2005. "Titanium Bar Details." http://www.el-cel.com/info/items_detail.php?Det=69, (accessed June 3, 2008).

Gladwell, M. 2013. *David and Goliath: Underdogs, Misfits, and the Art of Battling Giants*. New York, NY: Little, Brown and Company.

Gladwell, M. 2008. *Outliers: The Story of Success*. New York, NY: Little, Brown and Company.

Godin, S. 2003. *Purple Cow: Transform Your Business by Being Remarkable*. New York, NY: Penguin Group.

Gohan. April 27, 2006. "RE: A New Age Dawns, The Memoir of Mr.Mind [Online forum comment]." http://www.eternal-lands.com/forum/index.php?/topic/24738-a-new-age-dawns/&do=findComment&comment=261232, (accessed June 3, 2008).

Goodman, G.J.W. 1981. "Commanding Heights: The German Hyperinflation, 1923." http://www.pbs.org/wgbh/commandingheights/shared/minitext/ess_germanhyperinflation.html, (accessed June 23, 2018).

Google. June 28, 2018. "Eternal Lands." https://trends.google.com/trends/explore?date=all&q=%2Fm%2F06002p, (accessed June 28, 2018).

Google. June 28, 2018. "Massively Multiplayer Online Game." https://trends.google.com/trends/explore?q=%2Fm%2F02lzy0&date=all, (accessed June 28, 2018).

Google. June 28, 2018. "MMO." https://trends.google.com/trends/explore? date=all&q=MMO, (accessed June 28, 2018).

Grove, A.S. 1999. *Only the Paranoid Survive: How to Exploit the Crisis Points That Challenge Every Company.* New York, NY: Doubleday.

Hazor. February 6, 2004. "RE: I Would Like to Know the General Prices. [Online forum comment]." http://www.eternal-lands.com/forum/index.php?/ topic/2065-i-would-like-to-know-the-general-prices/&do= findComment&comment=16798, (accessed April 19, 2018).

History.com. 2009. "Ford's Assembly Line Starts Rolling." https://www.history.com/ this-day-in-history/fords-assembly-line-starts-rolling, (accessed March 21, 2018).

Hunter, J.D. 2000. The Death of Character: Moral Education in an Age Without Good or Evil. New York, NY: Basic Books.

Investopedia. n.d. "Baby Bells." https://www.investopedia.com/terms/b/baby-bells.asp, (accessed June 28, 2018).

Isaacson, W. 2011. *Steve Jobs.* New York, NY: Simon & Schuster.

Iskyan, K May 16, 2016. "How to Make, and Lose, Billions of Dollars in Silver." https://web.archive.org/web/20180121092506/http://stansberrychurchouse .com/asia-wealth-investment-daily/how-to-make-and-lose-billions-of-dollars-in-silver/, (accessed March 29, 2018).

jamesvm. January 12, 2005. "Selling Steel Chain Armour [Online forum comment]." http://www.eternal-lands.com/forum/index.php?/topic/11113-selling-steel-chain-armour/, (accessed June 27, 2018).

Kahneman, D. 2011. *Thinking, Fast and Slow.* New York, NY: Farrar, Straus and Giroux.

Kala. March 28, 2005. "RE: hEaL Mebers and Allies [Online forum comment]." http://www.eternal-lands.com/forum/index.php?/topic/13431-heal-mebers-and-allies/&do=findComment&comment=147892, (accessed July 20, 2010).

Kendai. April 28, 2006. "RE: A New Age Dawns, The Memoir of Mr.Mind [Online forum comment]." http://www.eternal-lands.com/forum/index.php?/ topic/24738-a-new-age-dawns/&do=findComment&comment=261477, (accessed June 3, 2008).

Knowledge@Wharton. March 14, 2012. "Vertical Integration Works for Apple—But It Won't for Everyone." http://knowledge.wharton.upenn.edu/article/ vertical-integration-works-for-apple-but-it-wont-for-everyone/, (accessed August 21, 2018).

Kouzes, J., and B. Posner. 2003. *Credibility: How Leaders Gain and Lose It, Why People Demand It.* San Francisco, CA: Jossey-Bass.

Kuhn, T.S. 1996. *The Structure of Scientific Revolutions.* 3rd. Chicago, IL: The University of Chicago Press.

LadyWolf. September 29, 2005. "RE: Crafter's Strike, Crafter's Strike and Why You Should Join [Online forum comment]." http://www.eternal-lands.com/forum/index.php?/topic/18519-crafters-strike/&do=findComment&comment=202926, (accessed November 29, 2008).

LadyWolf.September29,2005. "RE:Crafter'sStrike,Crafter'sStrikeAndWhyYouShould Join [Online forum comment]." http://www.eternal-lands.com/forum/index.php?/topic/18519-crafters-strike/&do=findComment&comment=202804, (accessed November 29, 2008).

LadyWolf.September29,2005. "RE:Crafter'sStrike,Crafter'sStrikeandWhyYouShould Join [Online forum comment]." http://www.eternal-lands.com/forum/index.php?/topic/18519-crafters-strike/&do=findComment&comment=202765, (accessed November 29, 2008).

Learner. December 22, 2003. "Silver, Alchemy, and Money [Online forum comment]." http://www.eternal-lands.com/forum/index.php?/topic/711-silver-alchemy-and-money/, (accessed August 22, 2018).

Leeloo. February 2004, 2004. "RE: Depot [Online forum comment]." http://www.eternal-lands.com/forum/index.php?/topic/3024-depot/&do=findComment&comment=24512, (accessed August 11, 2018).

Lewis, M. 2010. *The Big Short: Inside the Doomsday Machine.* New York, NY: W. W. Norton & Company.

Lewis, M. 2000. *The New New Thing: A Silicon Valley Story.* New York, NY: Penguin Books.

Lightning. January 7, 2004. "Discount Prices [Online forum comment]." http://www.eternal-lands.com/forum/index.php?/topic/1078-discount-prices/, (accessed April 19, 2018).

Little, K. October 31, 2016. "One Year after Chipotle's *E. coli* Crisis, Chain still Struggling." https://www.cnbc.com/2016/10/31/one-year-after-chipotles-e-coli-crisis-chain-still-struggling.html, (accessed March 21, 2018).

Llewellyn, J., J. Southey, and S. Thompson. 2014. "The 1923 Hyperinflation." http://alphahistory.com/weimarrepublic/1923-hyperinflation/, (accessed April 19, 2018).

llsardonicll. November 19, 2005. "RE: Manu Services [Online forum comment]." http://www.eternal-lands.com/forum/index.php?/topic/20190-manu-services/&do=findComment&comment=220717, (accessed June 23, 2018).

LochnessLobster. June 4, 2005. "Join Manu's On Strike! [Online forum comment]." http://www.eternal-lands.com/forum/index.php?/topic/15227-join-manus-on-strike/, (accessed November 29, 2008).

LochnessLobster. November 14, 2005. "Manu Services [Online forum comment]." http://www.eternal-lands.com/forum/index.php?/topic/20190-manu-services/, (accessed June 23, 2018).

LochnessLobster. September 29, 2005. "RE: Crafter's Strike, Crafter's Strike and Why You Should Join [Online forum comment]." http://www.eternal-lands.com/forum/index.php?/topic/18519-crafters-strike/&do=findComment&comment=202722, (accessed November 29, 2008).

LochnessLobster. June 10, 2005. "RE: Join Manu's On Strike! [Online forum comment]." http://www.eternal-lands.com/forum/index.php?/topic/15227-join-manus-on-strike/&do=findComment&comment=169389, (accessed November 29, 2008).

Lorck. September 30, 2005. "RE: RICH Services [Online forum comment]." http://www.eternal-lands.com/forum/index.php?/topic/16560-rich-services/&do=findComment&comment=203181, (accessed March 29, 2018).

MagpieLee. April 28, 2006. "RE: A New Age Dawns, The Memoir of Mr.Mind [Online forum comment]." http://www.eternal-lands.com/forum/index.php?/topic/24738-a-new-age-dawns/&do=findComment&comment=261512, (accessed June 3, 2008).

Mateer, D. n.d. "Opportunity Cost in "Joyce's Checkout"—Extreme Couponing." http://www.criticalcommons.org/Members/gdmateer/commentaries/opportunity-cost-in-joyces-checkout-extreme-couponing, (accessed August 21, 2018).

mauriciom. November 1, 2005. "Market Prices Are Going Down and Down [Online forum comment]." http://www.eternal-lands.com/forum/index.php?/topic/19845-market-prices-are-going-down-and-down/, (accessed November 29, 2008).

McGonigal, J. 2011. *Reality Is Broken: Why Games Make Us Better and How They Can Change the World.* New York ,NY: Penguin Books.

MoonShadow, Roja, and Tropicano. June 8, 2004. "Body Armor." https://web.archive.org/web/20040608105324/http:/eternal-lands.com:80/index.php?content=items_bodyarmor, (accessed August 11, 2018).

MoonShadow, Roja, and Tropicano. February 7, 2005. "Guild List." https://web.archive.org/web/20050207043850/http:/www.eternal-lands.com:80/index.php?content=guild_list, (accessed August 11, 2018).

MoonShadow, Roja, and Tropicano. May 19, 2005. "Guild List." https://web.archive.org/web/20050519090752/http:/www.eternal-lands.com:80/index.php?content=guild_list, (accessed August 11, 2018).

MoonShadow, Roja, and Tropicano. June 7, 2005. "Guild List." https://web.archive.org/web/20050607082606/http:/eternal-lands.com:80/index.php?content=guild_list, (accessed August 11, 2018).

MoonShadow, Roja, and Tropicano. March 6, 2004. "Shields." https://web.archive.org/web/20040306204449/http:/www.eternal-lands.com:80/index.php?content=items_shields, (accessed August 11, 2018).

MoonShadow, Roja, and Tropicano. June 8, 2004. "Shields." https://web. archive.org/web/20040608134731/http:/eternal-lands.com:80/index. php?content=items_shields, (accessed August 11, 2018).

MoonShadow, Roja, and Tropicano. March 6, 2004. *SWORDS.* https://web. archive.org/web/20040306205212/http:/www.eternal-lands.com:80/index. php?content=items_swords, (accessed August 11, 2018).

MoonShadow, Roja, and Tropicano. June 8, 2004. "Swords." https://web. archive.org/web/20040608140004/http:/eternal-lands.com:80/index. php?content=items_swords, (accessed August 11, 2018).

Mr.Mind. April 26, 2006. "A New Age Dawns, The Memoir of Mr.Mind [Online forum comment]." http://www.eternal-lands.com/forum/index.php?/ topic/24738-a-new-age-dawns/, (accessed June 3, 2008).

Mr.Mind. July 19, 2007. "Disappearing Money? [Online forum comment]." http://www.rich-guild.org.uk/hosted/richforum/viewtopic.php?f=22&t= 158&sid=024be03c4b1acc15d7bfbe1c4fef5153, (accessed June 28, 2018).

Mr.Mind. August 13, 2007. "I'm Leaving, for Good This Time. [Online forum comment]." http://www.rich-guild.org.uk/hosted/richforum/viewtopic.php? f=6&t=263&sid=c85ac02015f66b022f39fb1cdb272f14, (accessed June 28, 2018).

Mr.Mind. November 18, 2005. "Manu/Craft Items Sale." http://www.eternal-lands.com/forum/index.php?/topic/20170-manucraft-items-sale/&do=find Comment&comment=220534, (accessed June 27, 2018).

Mr.Mind. December 25, 2005. "Mass Production? [Online forum comment]." http://www.eternal-lands.com/forum/index.php?/topic/21290-mass-produ ction/&do=findComment&comment=229794, (accessed June 23, 2018).

Mr.Mind. September 28, 2005. "RE: Crafter's Strike, Crafter's Strike and Why You Should Join [Online forum comment]." http:// www.eternal-lands.com/forum/index.php?/topic/18519-crafters-strike/&do=findComment&comment=202527, (accessed November 29, 2008).

Mr.Mind. October 28, 2005. "RE: Enriched Fire Essence [Online forum comment]." http://www.eternal-lands.com/forum/index.php?/topic/19629-enriched-fire-essence/&do=findComment&comment=214810, (accessed June 27, 2018).

Mr.Mind. June 7, 2005. "RE: Join Manu's On Strike! [Online forum comment]." http://www.eternal-lands.com/forum/index.php?/topic/15227-join-manus-on-strike/&do=findComment&comment=168567, (accessed November 29, 2008).

Mr.Mind. October 1, 2005. "RE: RICH Services [Online forum comment]." http://www.eternal-lands.com/forum/index.php?/topic/16560-rich-services/&do=findComment&comment=203850, (accessed March 29, 2018).

Mr.Mind. October 1, 2005. "RE: RICH Services [Online forum comment]." http://www.eternal-lands.com/forum/index.php?/topic/16560-rich-services/&do=findComment&comment=203575, (accessed March 29, 2018).

Mr.Mind. September 30, 2005. "RE: RICH Services [Online forum comment]." http://www.eternal-lands.com/forum/index.php?/topic/16560-rich-services/&do=findComment&comment=203145, (accessed March 29, 2018).

Mr.Mind. September 29, 2005. "RE: RICH Services [Online forum comment]." http://www.eternal-lands.com/forum/index.php?/topic/16560-rich-services/&do=findComment&comment=202985, (accessed March 29, 2018).

Mr.Mind. July 21, 2005. "RICH Services [Online forum comment]." http://www.eternal-lands.com/forum/index.php?/topic/16560-rich-services/, (accessed March 29, 2018).

Mr.Mind. July 24, 2005. "richery [Online forum comment]." http://www.eternal-lands.com/forum/index.php?/topic/16625-richery/, (accessed October 25, 2016).

Mr.Mind. May 12, 2005. "Selling Steel Shields [Online forum comment]." http://www.eternal-lands.com/forum/index.php?/topic/14692-selling-steel-shields/, (accessed June 27, 2018).

Mr.Mind. July 26, 2007. "TirunCollimdus, A Record of Nasty Behavior [Online forum comment]." http://www.eternal-lands.com/forum/index.php?showtopic=36026?st=0, (accessed May 3, 2009).

Mulligan, J., and B. Patrovsky. 2003. *Developing Online Games: An Insider's Guide*. Indianapolis, IN: New Riders.

Mundaus. April 30, 2006. "RE: A New Age Dawns, The Memoir of Mr.Mind [Online forum comment]." http://www.eternal-lands.com/forum/index.php?/topic/24738-a-new-age-dawns/&do=findComment&comment=261978, (accessed June 3, 2008).

Nidan. April 28, 2006. "RE: A New Age Dawns, The Memoir of Mr.Mind [Online forum comment]." http://www.eternal-lands.com/forum/index.php?/topic/24738-a-new-age-dawns/&do=findComment&comment=261281, (accessed June 3, 2008).

Octane. April 27, 2006. "RE: A New Age Dawns, The Memoir of Mr.Mind [Online forum comment]." http://www.eternal-lands.com/forum/index.php?/topic/24738-a-new-age-dawns/&do=findComment&comment=261236, (accessed June 3, 2008).

Olson, R. November 12, 2014. "MMORPG Popularity, 1998-2013." http://www.randalolson.com/2014/11/12/mmorpg-popularity-1998-2013/, (accessed April 19, 2018).

OPEC. 2018. "Member Countries." http://www.opec.org/opec_web/en/about_ us/25.htm, (accessed March 22, 2018).

OPEC. 2017. "OPEC Share of World Crude Oil Reserves." http://www.opec. org/opec_web/en/data_graphs/330.htm, (accessed March 22, 2018).

Pagliery, J. May 20, 2014. "How AT&T Got Busted Up and Pieced Back To- gether." http://money.cnn.com/2014/05/20/technology/att-merger-history/ index.html, (accessed June 28, 2018).

Pausch, R. September 18, 2007. "Randy Pausch Last Lecture: Achieving Your Child- hood Dreams." https://youtu.be/ji5_MqicxSo, (accessed November 29, 2008).

Phenic. November 1, 2005. "RE: Market Prices Are Going Down and Down [Online forum comment]." http://www.eternal-lands.com/forum/index. php?/topic/19845-market-prices-are-going-down-and-down/&do=findCo mment&comment=216007, (accessed November 29, 2008).

Placid. July 24, 2005. "RE: Richery [Online forum comment]." http:// www.eternal-lands.com/forum/index.php?/topic/16625-richery/ &do=findComment&comment=182651, (accessed October 25, 2016).

Privantu, R. November 24, 2004. "Eternal Lands' MMORPG Postmortem: Mis- takes and Lessons, Part I." https://web.archive.org/web/20070108063342/ http://www.devmaster.net/articles/mmorpg-postmortem/part1.php, (accessed November 26, 2009).

Privantu, R. May 14, 2006. "Some Things to Expect in EL Soon [Blog]." http:// eternal-lands.blogspot.com/2006/05/some-things-to-expect-in-el-soon. html, (accessed November 26, 2009).

Razvan21. March 5, 2005. "Selling Irong Helms [Online forum comment]." http://www.eternal-lands.com/forum/index.php?/topic/12697-selling- irong-helms/, (accessed June 27, 2018).

Roja, and Ghrae. April 23, 2007. "Guilds of Eternal Lands." https://web.archive. org/web/20070423144536/http:/www.eternal-lands.com:80/page/guild_ list.php, (accessed August 11, 2018).

Roja, Ghrae, mihaim, and Learner. April 6, 2006. "top200." https://web.archive. org/web/20060406074248/http:/www.other-life.com:80/el/top/top200. php, (accessed August 11, 2018).

Roja, Ghrae, mihaim, and Learner. July 16, 2006. "top200." https://web.archive. org/web/20060716015434/http:/www.other-life.com:80/el/top/top200. php, (accessed August 11, 2018).

Roja, Ghrae, mihaim, and Learner. December 11, 2006. "top200." https://web. archive.org/web/20061211143024/http:/www.other-life.com:80/el/top/ top200.php, (accessed August 11, 2018).

Schick, L. 1991. *Heroic Worlds: A History And Guide to Role-Playing Games*. Buf- falo, NY: Prometheus Books.

seanodonnell. April 1, 2005. "RE: hEaL Mebers and Allies [Online forum comment]." http://www.eternal-lands.com/forum/index.php?/topic/13431-heal-mebers-and-allies/&do=findComment&comment=149159, (accessed July 20, 2010).

seanodonnell. April 1, 2005. "RE: hEaL Mebers and Allies [Online forum comment]." http://www.eternal-lands.com/forum/index.php?/topic/13431-heal-mebers-and-allies/&do=findComment&comment=149056, (accessed July 20, 2010).

Shell, A. August 2, 2018. "Apple makes history by becoming first US company to reach $1 trillion market value." https://www.usatoday.com/story/money/2018/08/02/apple-first-stock-hit-1-trillion-market-value/877867002/, (accessed August 21, 2018).

Shoop, R.J., and S.M. Scott. 1999. *Leadership Lessons from Bill Snyder*. Manhattan, KS: AG Press.

SiKiK. January 16, 2006. "Crapola Spreadsheet." http://www.aozt61.dsl.pipex.com/richery.html, (accessed June 23, 2018).

SiKiK. April 29, 2006. "RE: A New Age Dawns, The Memoir of Mr.Mind [Online forum comment]." http://www.eternal-lands.com/forum/index.php?/topic/24738-a-new-age-dawns/&do=findComment&comment=261712, (accessed June 3, 2008).

Sloan, S. 2000. *Digital Fictions: Storytelling in a Material World*. Stamford, CT: Ablex Publishing Corporation.

Smith, A. 1994. *The Wealth of Nations*. New York, NY: Random House.

Sorkin, A.R. 2009. *Too Big to Fail: The Inside Story of How Wall Street and Washington Fought to Save the Financial System—and Themselves*. New York, NY: Penguin Group.

Tedlow, R.S. 2001. *Giants of Enterprise: Seven Business Innovators and the Empires They Built*. New York, NY: HarperCollins Publishers.

Thaler, R.H., and C.R. 2009. Sunstein. *Nudge: Improving Decisions About Health, Wealth, and Happiness*. London, England: Penguin Books.

the_antiroot. April 29, 2006. "RE: A New Age Dawns, The Memoir of Mr.Mind [Online forum comment]." http://www.eternal-lands.com/forum/index.php?/topic/24738-a-new-age-dawns/&do=findComment&comment=261682, (accessed June 3, 2008).

the_antiroot. April 28, 2006. "RE: A New Age Dawns, The Memoir of Mr.Mind [Online forum comment]." http://www.eternal-lands.com/forum/index.php?/topic/24738-a-new-age-dawns/&do=findComment&comment=261364, (accessed June 3, 2008).

TheDoctor. September 29, 2005. "RE: Crafter's Strike, Crafter's Strike and why You Should Join [Online forum comment]." http://www.eternal-lands.com/forum/index.php?/topic/18519-crafters-strike/&do=findComment&comment=202986, (accessed November 29, 2008).

TirunCollimdus. November 14, 2007. "Leaving the PATH. [Online forum comment]." http://www.eternal-lands.com/forum/index.php?/topic/38439-leaving-the-path/, (accessed June 29, 2018).

TirunCollimdus. February 20, 2009. "RE: Is My Character Locked? [Online forum comment]." http://www.eternal-lands.com/forum/index.php?/topic/48489-is-my-character-locked/&page=2&tab=comments#comment-488648, (accessed June 29, 2018).

TirunCollimdus. October 1, 2010. "RE: TirunCollimdus, a Record of Nasty Behavior [Online forum comment]." (accessed November 11, 2016).

Torg. April 27, 2006. "RE: A New Age Dawns, The Memoir of Mr.Mind [Online forum comment]." http://www.eternal-lands.com/forum/index.php?/topic/24738-a-new-age-dawns/&do=findComment&comment=261261, (accessed June 3, 2008).

Torg. June 9, 2009. "Trinitybot Price Database."

trollson. April 6, 2006. "Dacia—Price List and Stocks [Online forum comment]." https://web.archive.org/web/20060430193837/http:/richtimothy.com:80/index.php?action=recent, (accessed June 27, 2018).

trollson. July 10, 2007. "EL Market Prices (Google Spreadsheet) [Online forum comment]."

trollson. April 27, 2006. "RE: Fixing Some of the Economy [Online forum comment]." http://www.eternal-lands.com/forum/index.php?/topic/24624-fixing-some-of-the-economy/&page=7&tab=comments#comment-261093, (accessed November 29, 2008).

trollson. April 25, 2006. "RE: Fixing Some of the Economy [Online forum comment]." http://www.eternal-lands.com/forum/index.php?/topic/24624-fixing-some-of-the-economy/&page=2&tab=comments#comment-260433, (accessed November 29, 2008).

trollson. June 30, 2006. "RE: Fixing Some of the Economy [Online forum comment]." http://www.eternal-lands.com/forum/index.php?/topic/24624-fixing-some-of-the-economy/&page=10&tab=comments#comment-278450, (accessed November 29, 2008).

trollson. June 18, 2005. "RE: Manu Price List [Online forum comment]." http://www.eternal-lands.com/forum/index.php?/topic/15333-manu-price-list/&do=findComment&comment=171643, (accessed June 27, 2018).

trollson. July 25, 2005. "RE: Richery [Online forum comment]." http://www.eternal-lands.com/forum/index.php?/topic/16625-richery/&do=findComment&comment=182849, (accessed October 25, 2016).

trollson. July 24, 2005. "RE: Richery [Online forum comment]." http://www.eternal-lands.com/forum/index.php?/topic/16625-richery/&do=findComment&comment=182712, (accessed October 25, 2016).

ttlanhil. April 28, 2006. "RE: A New Age Dawns, The Memoir of Mr.Mind [Online forum comment]." http://www.eternal-lands.com/forum/index.php?/

topic/24738-a-new-age-dawns/&do=findComment&comment=261274, (accessed June 3, 2008).

ttlanhil. January 1, 2006. "RE: How Many People Play el? [Online forum comment]." http://www.eternal-lands.com/forum/index.php?/topic/21393-how-many-people-play-el/&do=findComment&comment=231257, (accessed June 27, 2018).

ttlanhil. September 30, 2005. "RE: RICH Services [Online forum comment]." http://www.eternal-lands.com/forum/index.php?/topic/16560-rich-services/&do=findComment&comment=203027, (accessed March 29, 2018).

ttlanhil. September 30, 2005. "RE: RICH Services [Online forum comment]." http://www.eternal-lands.com/forum/index.php?/topic/16560-rich-services/&do=findComment&comment=203071, (accessed March 29, 2018).

valo13. April 1, 2005. "RE: hEaL Mebers and Allies [Online forum comment]." http://www.eternal-lands.com/forum/index.php?/topic/13431-heal-mebers-and-allies/&do=findComment&comment=148984, (accessed July 20, 2010).

valo13. March 28, 2005. "RE: hEaL Mebers and Allies [Online forum comment]." http://www.eternal-lands.com/forum/index.php?/topic/13431-heal-mebers-and-allies/&do=findComment&comment=147891, (accessed July 20, 2010).

valo13. March 29, 2005. "RE: hEaL Mebers and Allies [Online forum comment]." http://www.eternal-lands.com/forum/index.php?/topic/13431-heal-mebers-and-allies/&do=findComment&comment=147913, (accessed July 20, 2010).

vampireLOREN. April 28, 2006. "RE: A New Age Dawns, The Memoir of Mr.Mind [Online forum comment]." http://www.eternal-lands.com/forum/index.php?/topic/24738-a-new-age-dawns/&do=findComment&comment=261384, (accessed June 3, 2008).

Wagner, A. 2012. The Economic Consequences of Network Neutrality Regulation. Master's report, Kansas State University.

Wall, J.F. 1989. *Andrew Carnegie*. Pittsburgh, PA: University of Pittsburgh Press.

Walton, S., and J. Huey. 1993. *Sam Walton: Made in America*. New York, NY: Bantam Books.

Weinberger, D. 2002. *Small Pieces Loosely Joined: A Unified Theory of the Web*. Cambridge, MA: Perseus Publishing.

Wheelan, C. 2010. *Naked Economics: Undressing the Dismal Science*. New York, NY: W. W. Norton & Company.

Wheeler, T. December 14, 2017. "A Goal Realized: Network Lobbyists' Sweeping Capture of Their Regulator." https://www.brookings.edu/blog/

techtank/2017/12/14/a-goal-realized-network-lobbyists-sweeping-capture-of-their-regulator/, (accessed May 30, 2018).

Thorndike, W.N., Jr. 2012. *The Outsiders: Eight Unconventional CEOs and Their Radically Rational Blueprint for Success.* Boston, MA: Harvard Business Review Press.

WoodeH. June 25, 2005. "Buying & Selling [Online forum comment]." http://www.eternal-lands.com/forum/index.php?/topic/15820-buying-selling/, (accessed June 30, 2018).

Zuckerman, G. 2009. *The Greatest Trade Ever: The Behind-the-Scenes Story of How John Paulson Defied Wall Street and Made Financial History.* New York, NY: Broadway Books.

About the Author

Andrew Wagner is a dedicated gamer and a passionate advocate for economics education. He is the founder and chief investment officer of Wagner Road Capital Management, LLC, a Minnesota-based registered investment adviser. Through his firm, he provides investment consulting services to professional fund managers and manages an investment fund that identifies and invests in high-quality companies. His professional experience covers consulting projects in a wide range of investment strategies, asset classes, and industries, and his ghost-written research has appeared in national and regional publications. He has a master's degree in economics from Kansas State University.

Index

OTHER TITLES FROM THE ECONOMICS AND PUBLIC POLICY COLLECTION

Philip Romero, The University of Oregon and
Jeffrey Edwards, North Carolina A&T State University, *Editors*

- *Macroeconomics, Second Edition, Volume I* by David G. Tuerck
- *Macroeconomics, Second Edition, Volume II* by David G. Tuerck
- *Economic Renaissance In the Age of Artificial Intelligence* by Apek Mulay
- *Disaster Risk Management: Case Studies in South Asian Countries*
  by Huong Ha, R. Lalitha S. Fernando, and Sanjeev Kumar Mahajan
- *The Option Strategy Desk Reference: An Essential Reference for Option Traders*
  by Russell A. Stultz
- *Disaster Risk Management in Agriculture: Case Studies in South Asian Countries*
  by Huong Ha, Lalitha S. Fernando and Sanjeev Kumar Mahajan
- *Understanding Demonetization in India: A Deft Stroke of Economic Policy*
  by Shrawan Kumar Singh
- *Urban Development 2120* by Peter Nelson
- *Foreign Direct Investment: The Indian Experience* by Leena Ajit Kaushal
- *A Guide to International Economics* by Shahruz Mohtadi
- *The Options Trading Primer: Using Rules-Based Option Trades to Earn a Steady Income*
  by Russell A. Stultz
- *Political Dimensions of the American Macroeconomy* by Gerald T. Fox
- *Global Sustainable Capitalism* by Marcus Goncalves, Mario Svigir and Harry Xia

Announcing the Business Expert Press Digital Library

Concise e-books business students need for classroom and research

This book can also be purchased in an e-book collection by your library as

- *a one-time purchase,*
- *that is owned forever,*
- *allows for simultaneous readers,*
- *has no restrictions on printing, and*
- *can be downloaded as PDFs from within the library community.*

Our digital library collections are a great solution to beat the rising cost of textbooks. E-books can be loaded into their course management systems or onto students' e-book readers. The **Business Expert Press** digital libraries are very affordable, with no obligation to buy in future years. For more information, please visit **www.businessexpertpress.com/librarians**. To set up a trial in the United States, please email **sales@businessexpertpress.com**.

www.ingramcontent.com/pod-product-compliance
Lightning Source LLC
Chambersburg PA
CBHW061221220326
41599CB00025B/4713